Codes, Ciphers, Steganography & Secret Messages

Copyright & Other Notices

Information about other books written by the same author can be found at
http://www.suniltanna.com/

For related resources and more information about codes, ciphers and secret messages go to
http://www.suniltanna.com/codes

Information about computing books by the same author can be found at
http://www.suniltanna.com/computing

Information about math books by the same author can be found at
http://www.suniltanna.com/math

Information about science books by the same author can be found at
http://www.suniltanna.com/science

Table of Contents

Grille Ciphers
- Trellis Ciphers
- Fleissner Ciphers
- Crossword Ciphers

Chapter 5: Fractionation and Diffusion
Bifid Cipher
Trifid Cipher

Chapter 6: Polygraphic Substitution
Advantages and Disadvantages of Polygraphic Ciphers
Playfair Cipher
Two-Square Cipher
Four-Square Cipher

Chapter 7: Polyalphabetic Ciphers
Alberti Cipher
Trithemius Cipher
Vigenère Ciphers
Beaufort and Variant Beaufort Cipher
Autokey Ciphers

Chapter 8: Enigma
The Enigma Machine
How Enigma was Broken
- Early British Efforts
- Polish Cipher Bureau
- Polish Cooperation with the Western Allies
- PC Bruno
- Cadix
- British Efforts Against Italian Naval Enigma
- The British Focus on Cribs
- British and American Bombes
- German Suspicions

Chapter 9: Perfect Ciphers
Vernam Cipher
One-Time Pads
Difficulties of Implementing a Perfect Cipher

- Protecting the Key
- Not Reusing the Key
- Randomness in the Key
- The Equipment Used Must Be Secure

Lorenz Cipher
- Cryptanalysis of the Lorenz Cipher

Chapter 10: Codewords
One-time Code
Nomenclator
Midway

Chapter 11: Book Ciphers
Book Word Substitution Ciphers
Book Letter Substitution Ciphers
Running Key Ciphers

Chapter 12: Computer Cryptography
Symmetric-Key Cryptography
Public-Key Cryptography
Cryptographic Hashes and Digital Signatures

Chapter 13: Steganography and Hidden Messages
Null Ciphers
Bacon's Cipher
Grilles
Digital Steganography

- Image Files
- Audio Files
- Text and Word Processor Files
- Network Communications
- Other Examples

Chapter 14: Famous Codes, Ciphers and Cryptograms – Solved and Unsolved
Voynich Manuscript
Babington Plot Ciphers
Olivier Levasseur
Shugborough Inscription
Copiale Cipher
The Gold-Bug
Beale Ciphers
Rohonc Codex
D'Agapeyeff Cipher
Dorabella Cipher
Zimmerman Telegram
Zodiac Killer Ciphers
Kryptos
The Magic Words are Squeamish Ossifrage
Ricky McCormick's Encrypted Notes
Smithy Code

Conclusion

Introduction: What are Codes, Ciphers and Steganography?

This book is about codes, ciphers, and steganography. What are each of these?

A **code** is a system of rules for converting letters, words, images, sounds, gestures, etc., into another form that represents the same information. For example, Morse code (see Chapter 1) allows letters to be represented as pulses of light, sound or electricity. Similarly, semaphore code (also described in Chapter 1) allows letters to represented as movements of signal flags. There are of course many other types of codes.

- The process of converting information from its original form into a code is called **encoding**.
- The process of converting information from its coded form back to original form is called **decoding**.
- If the method of encoding and decoding information to/from the code is kept secret, codes can be used as a means of confidentially communicating, however this is usually **not** the case.

US Navy Signalman using semaphore to communicate:

A **cipher** (also sometimes written **cypher**) is a series of well-defined steps (an **algorithm**) for converting a message into a format that only authorized parties can read, and later converting back.

- The original message is known as the **plaintext**.
- The message in a secret form that only authorized parties can read is called the **ciphertext**.
- An entire message in ciphertext is called a **cryptogram**.
- The process of converting plaintext to ciphertext is known as **enciphering** or **encryption**.
- The process of converting ciphertext back to plaintext is known as **deciphering** or **decryption**.

- The study of codes and ciphers is called **cryptology**. The people who study cryptology are called **cryptologists**.
- The study of creating and using codes and ciphers is called **cryptography**. The people who study cryptography are called **cryptographers**.
- While the purpose of ciphers is to prevent unauthorized people from deciphering the ciphertext, ciphers are **<u>not</u>** always successful in this goal. Sometimes it is possible for a clever adversary to figure out how to decipher cryptograms. This is known as **cryptanalysis** (or informally as **codebreaking**), and a person engaged in cryptanalysis is known as a **cryptanalyst** (or informally as a **codebreaker**).

Enigma (see Chapter 8) was an electromechanical machine that enciphered and deciphered messages. It was used by Germany in the interwar years and during World War II.

Steganography is the practice of concealing information such as text, an image, a video, or computer data within other information, such as text, an image, a video, or computer data. For example, a paragraph of text might contain a message hidden within it, or a graphical image on a computer screen can contain text hidden within very subtle variations in color within the picture. Some examples of steganography that have been used in the past include invisible inks and writing messages on the envelopes of letters in the area that is covered by the postage stamps.

Benedict Arnold used codes and steganography to communicate with the British during the American Revolutionary War. His coded messages were written in invisible ink (though now visible) and interspersed between the lines of an apparently normal letter written by his wife, Peggy Shippen Arnold.

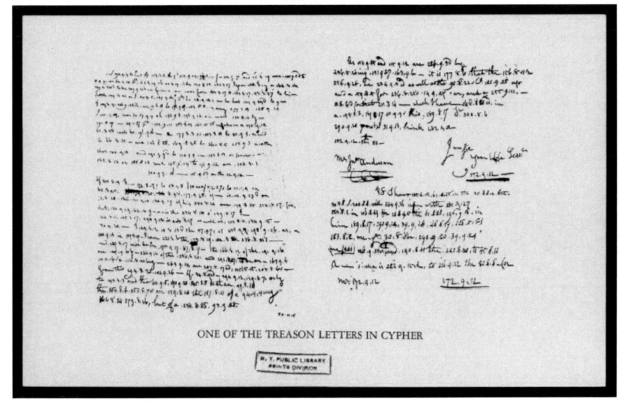

ONE OF THE TREASON LETTERS IN CYPHER

Chapter 1: Codes used for Communication

Codes are widely used in communication. For example, if we want messages to be readable from a great distance, a greater distance than letters would be visible, we could send the message in flag code or semaphore code. Similarly, if we want to send messages via an electrical circuit, codes that encode letters and digits as electrical pulses can be used.

By themselves, these codes are **not** useful for sending secret messages, because the details of how each code works are generally widely known and published. This means that anybody intercepting a coded message can potentially decode and read it.

However, codes can be used in combination with a cipher (ciphers are described in detail in later chapters) to send secret messages:

- The sender uses a cipher to convert a plaintext message into ciphertext.
- The sender encodes the ciphertext and transmits the encoded ciphertext.
- The recipient decodes the encoded ciphertext to retrieve the ciphertext
- The recipient deciphers the ciphertext to obtain the plaintext.
- Anybody who intercepts the message in transit will only obtain the encoded ciphertext. They will probably be able to decode it to get the ciphertext, but they will **not** be able to decipher the ciphertext to plaintext, and therefore will **not** be able to read the message.

Comparison of sending a message using a code (top) versus using a cipher and code (bottom):

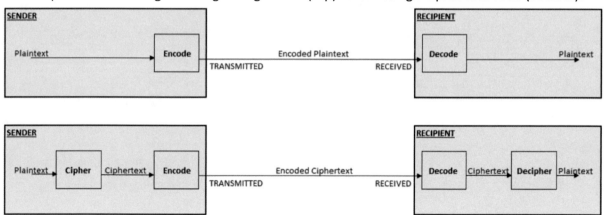

Flag Code

The **International Code of Signals** (ICS) is a standard using for communicating in maritime environment, especially by ships. The standard is maintained by the International Maritime Organization (IMO), a specialized United Nations agency, which is responsible for regulating shipping.

ICS allows messages to be communicated by flags, semaphore, signal lamps ("blinker") and radio. The flag code specifies:

- Twenty-six colored flags corresponding to letters of the alphabet. For each letter there is also a phonetic word that can be used in radio communication, so for example the letter "B" is "Bravo", and the letter "H" is "Hotel".

- Ten flags corresponding to the digits "0" through "9".
- Three substitute flags which mean repeat the first, second or third letter of a message. The purpose of these flags is that a short message can be transmitted using flags, even if the message contains repeated letters, without the ship having to keep an inventory of flags with several copies of each letter.
- One special flag (known as the Code/Answer Pennant) that can be used to indicate when ready to a receive a message, that a message has been received, end of message, etc.

ICS flags:

ALPHABET FLAGS			NUMERAL PENNANTS
Alfa	Kilo	Uniform	1
Bravo	Lima	Victor	2
Charlie	Mike	Whis-key	3
Delta	Novem-ber	Xray	4
Echo	Oscar	Yankee	5
Foxtrot	Papa	Zulu	6
Golf	Quebec	SUBSTITUTES 1st Substitute	7
Hotel	Romeo	2nd Substitute	8
India	Sierra	3rd Substitute	9
Juliett	Tango	CODE (Answering Pennant or Decimal Point)	0

As well as the letter code, certain short abbreviations have standard meanings. So, for example, the "D" or "Delta" flag flown alone used to indicate that the ship is maneuvering with difficulty and other vessels should keep clear, the "K" or "Kilo" flag is used to indicate a wish to communicate, and the combination "MAA" is used to request urgent medical assistance.

"MAA" is encoded by hoisting the flags for "Mike", "Alfa", and then "2nd Substitute" (meaning repeat the second letter):

Semaphore Code

Semaphore is a means of sending information at a distance using visual signals. Each signal is conveyed by the position of the sender's two hands and encodes a letter or a digit, or has a special meaning such as indicating an error, cancel the last signal, etc. It is **not** necessary to hold an object in the hands when sending a semaphore signal, but it is usual to hold a flag, rod, paddle or disk, in order to make the signal more visible. Square flags with short poles are normally used: red and yellow flags (the Oscar flag) when sending messages at sea, and white and blue flags (the Papa flag) when sending messages on land.

Semaphore alphabet:

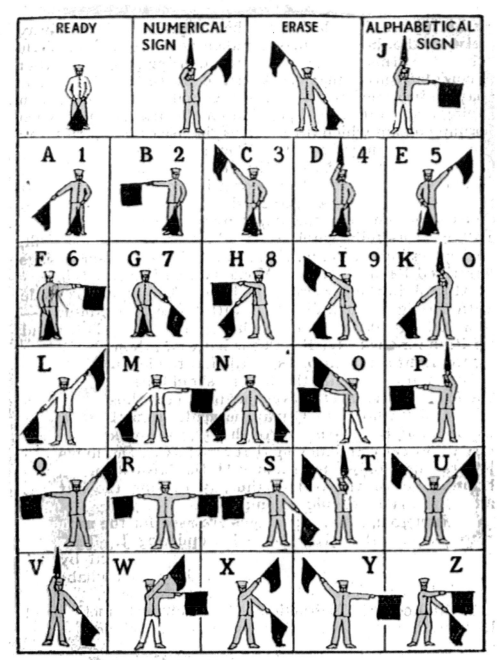

Polybius Square

The **Polybius square** (also known as the **Polybius checkerboard**) is a grid on which letters are laid out, and which can be used to encode a letter of the alphabet as a pair of digits. The device was developed by the Ancient Greeks: it was originally created by two Greek engineers from Alexandria in Egypt (Cleoxenus and Democleitus), and then subsequently improved by Polybius (c. 208 BC to c. 125 BC) who described in his famous work, *The Histories*.

In the Polybius square, the alphabet is laid out across a grid of cells, and each letter can be referenced by the coordinates of the cell containing the letter.

- The Ancient Greeks used an alphabet with 24 letters, so were able to accommodate all the letters within a 5×5 square, still leaving one square unused.
- For English, it is also normal to use a 5×5 square, and the fact that the alphabet has 26 letters can be dealt with by treating two letters as equivalent (normally "I" and "J", but sometimes "C" and "K", or sometimes "K" and "Q").
- For languages that use a Cyrillic alphabet (with between 33 and 37 letters), a 6×6 Polybius square is normally used.

Greek Polybius Square:

	1	2	3	4	5
1	A	B	Γ	Δ	E
2	Z	H	Θ	I	K
3	Λ	M	N	Ξ	O
4	Π	P	Σ	T	Y
5	Φ	X	Ψ	Ω	

English Polybius Square:

	1	2	3	4	5
1	A	B	C	D	E
2	F	G	H	I,J	K
3	L	M	N	O	P
4	Q	R	S	T	U
5	V	W	X	Y	Z

The Ancient Greeks used the Polybius square as a means of visual telegraphy. A letter could be communicated by lighting torches and displaying them in two groups. The number of torches in one group would indicate the row number of the letter, and the number of torches in the other group would indicate the column number of the letter.

Other uses of Polybius squares include audible and tactile knocks ("knock codes") used by prisoners to communicate without knowledge of their guards, as well as to secretly communicate messages using stenography (see Chapter 13) by for example placing knots on a string, stitches in embroidery, or even by varying the spacing or visual appearance of letters in text. Additionally, since a Polybius square can be used to encode letters into numbers, which can then be further manipulated, there are many ciphers which take advantage of this feature of Polybius squares.

Optical Telegraph Codes

We have already seen how semaphore and Polybius square can be used to transmit messages using visual signals. Later inventions built on these ideas to develop optical telegraph systems.

The first practical optical telegraph system was developed in late 18th century France by Claude Chappe (December 25th, 1763 to January 23rd, 1805). The system was based on a system of towers all within line of sight (using a telescope) of each other. Each tower was equipped with a wooden mast with a pivoted beam and moveable arms. Messages were encoded into **Chappe code** by positioning the beam and arms in various configurations. The Chappe network eventually spanned across France and remained in use until the mid-19th century when it was replaced by the electrical telegraph.

Chappe code (left) and a typical Chappe communication station (right):

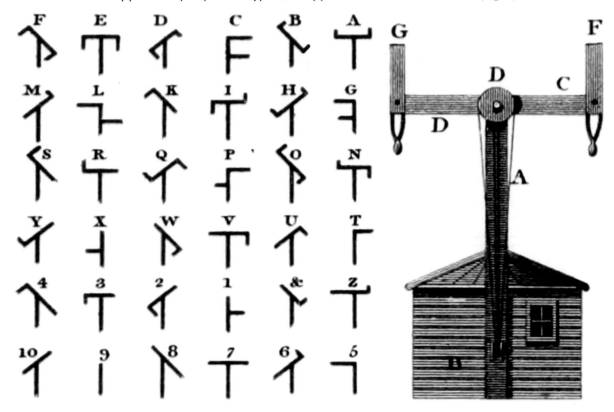

Other optical telegraph systems that were developed during the 19th century included:
- Sweden was the second country after France to build an optical telegraph network. The Swedish optical telegraph was called the **Edelcrantz system** and was based on ten shutters which could be individually opened or closed.
- In Britain, the Admiralty also developed a system based on array of shutters which could be individually opened or closed.
- In the 1850s, Albert J. Myer (September 20th, 1828 to August 24th, 1880) developed an optical communication system based on flag signals. The system which relied on the movement of a single flag came to be known as the **wig-wag method** of signaling. Wig-wag signaling was first used by the US Army in an 1860 campaign against the Navajo, and then extensively used by both sides during the American Civil War (1861 to 1865). Albert J. Myer

is today remembered as father of the US Army Signal Corps, and later helped found the US Weather Bureau (now part of the National Oceanic and Atmospheric Administration) and the International Meteorological Organization (now succeeded by the World Meteorological Organization).

Albert J. Myer:

Electrical Telegraph Codes

The earliest proposals for an electrical telegraph system were made as long ago as 1753, and the first experimental demonstration of such a system being used over a significant distance occurred in 1816. However, it was **not** until the 1830s that electrical telegraphs began to be used in practice.

Each early electrical telegraph system tended to have their own code devised by its inventor and suited to the apparatus used in that system.

- The first such code was **Cooke and Wheatstone telegraph five needle code (C&W5)**, which was introduced on the Great Western Railway in 1838. C&W5 had one big advantage over many other codes: the operator did not need to learn the code, but code simply read messages from a display board. However, C&W5 also required five wires between telegraph stations and was **not** commercially competitive because of this.
- A code that only required one wire, **Cooke and Wheatstone telegraph one needle code (C&W1)**, was also later developed. C&W1 was used in Great Britain and in some parts of the British Empire but never became an international standard.
- In France, the Foy-Breguet telegraph was developed by Louis François Clément Breguet (December 22nd, 1804 to October 27th, 1883) and Alphonse Foy (April 14th, 1796 to January 15th, 1888). This system used a two-needle system to produce a display similar to that of the Chappe optical telegraph system. This had the advantage that there was no need to retrain telegraph operators.
- In the United States, Samuel Morse (April 27th, 1791 to April 2nd, 1872) and Alfred Vail (September 25th, 1807 to January 18th, 1859) introduced **American Morse Code** (also known as **railroad code**). American Morse Code originally was intended to only encode digits, with combinations of numbers intended to reference a dictionary containing a limited set of words, but Alfred Vail extended the code to allow letters to also be encoded although

it did require three different length pulses and two different lengths of space to encode the characters supported.

Foy-Breguet telegraph display. The central pivot and the two attached arms are intended to resemble the optical signals used in the Chappe system:

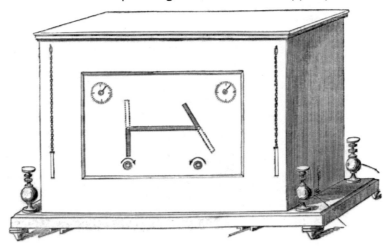

The problems of using multiple systems soon became apparent when messages were sent across borders. For example, a submarine telegraph cable was laid between France and England in 1851, but two operators were required at the English end: one who was familiar with the French Foy-Breguet system, and another who was familiar with the British Cooke and Wheatstone system.

Illustration of the use of submarine telegraphy in 1852. The Foy-Breguet display unit and the Cooke and Wheatstone unit can both be seen:

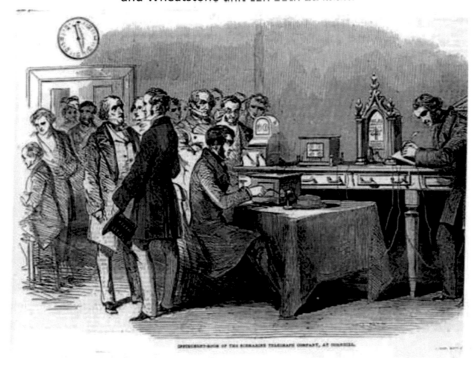

International Morse Code

In 1848, Friedrich Clemens Gerke (January 22nd, 1801 to May 21st, 1888) developed a revised version of Morse code for use on German railroads. Gerke's system was simplified from the original American system: there were now only two lengths of pulses (now generally called dots and dashes) as opposed to the original three. Additionally, Gerke's system only used a single gap length within letters and had codes for German umlaut letters.

Friedrich Clemens Gerke:

Gerke's code was adopted as a standard by the German-Austrian Telegraph Union in 1851 and thus came to be used across a range of central European countries (hence was commonly known as **continental code**). In 1865, Gerke's code became a recognized international standard known as **International Morse code**, and with only minor changes, remains so to this day.

International Morse code:

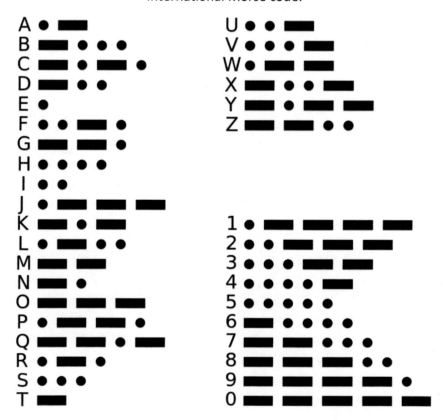

International Morse code is nowadays used in a wide variety of applications and transmission modes as well as telegraphy. For example, radio signals, visual signals such as flashing lights, and audible sounds can also be used to transmit messages in International Morse code.

US Navy Seaman sends a visual signal using International Morse code:

Baudot Code

In 1846, Royal Earl House (September 9th, 1814 to February 25th, 1895) invented the first printing telegraph. Early models continued to use Morse code, but instead of the operator keying in dots and dashes directly, he pressed a single key on a piano-like keyboard which then generated and transmitted the appropriate Morse code signal. At the other end of the telegraph line, the receiving equipment automatically printed the message on a slip of paper.

Printing telegraph machine on display in Stockholm, Sweden:

Early printing telegraphs required that the machines at both ends of the line be in perfect synchronization. In 1874, Émile Baudot (September 11th, 1845 to March 28th, 1903) introduced a new method of data transmission that overcome this limitation and also simplified machine design: **Baudot code**.

Émile Baudot:

Each character in Baudot code consists of five plus/minus (**binary**) signals known as **bits**. Each of the bits is sent one after another sequentially, with the overall combination of bits signifying the character encoded. Additionally, special start and stop bits are added to each character on transmission which means that transmitting and receiving equipment do **not** need to keep in synchronization – messages can be sent asynchronously.

Character encoding in Baudot code (from the 1888 US patent):

	1	2	3	4	5
A	+	−	−	−	−
B	−	−	+	+	−
C	+	−	+	+	−
D	+	+	+	+	−
E	−	+	−	−	−
F	+	+	−	−	−
G	−	+	+	+	−
H	+	+	−	+	−
I	−	+	+	−	−
J	+	−	−	+	−
K	+	−	−	+	+
L	+	+	−	+	+
M	−	+	−	+	+
N	−	+	+	+	+
O	+	+	+	−	−
P	+	+	+	−	+
Q	+	−	+	+	+
R	−	−	+	+	+
S	−	+	+	−	+
T	+	−	+	−	+
U	+	−	+	−	+
V	+	+	+	−	+
W	−	+	+	+	+
X	−	+	−	+	+
Y	−	−	+	−	+
Z	+	+	−	−	+
è	+	+	−	−	+
&	−	−	−	+	+
↑	−	−	−	+	+
	−	−	−	−	+
	−	−	−	−	−

Baudot code was originally entered by the operating using a special piano-like keyboard with five keys. Each key pressed corresponded to one bit in the signal, and in order to minimize operator fatigue, the most common letters were assigned those codes which were easiest to enter.

Early Baudot keyboard:

Murray Code and ITA 2

Murray code (sometimes called **Murray-Baudot code**) is a variant of Baudot code that was introduced in 1901 by Donald Murray (1865 to 1945), and later formed the basis of the widely used international standard, **International Telegraph Alphabet no. 2 (ITA 2)**.

Donald Murray:

In Murray code, like Baudot code, coded characters are each five bits long. Five bits however only allows a maximum of 32 combinations, which is **not** enough to represent all the letters, punctuation and special control characters (like linefeed to start a new line of text) that Murray realized were needed. To overcome this limitation, Murray used certain bit combinations as shift characters which had the effect of changing the meaning of subsequent characters. For example, in Murray code the letter "R" and the digit "4" are represented by exactly the same combination of bits, but we can tell which is being sent based on whether we are in letters mode or figures mode, which in turn is determined by whether the most recent preceding shift character was letter shift or figure shift.

ITA2 code assignments:
(shift characters are LeTteRS and FIGureS, control characters are BLANK, SPACE, STOP, BELL, CARriage RETurn and LINE FEED)

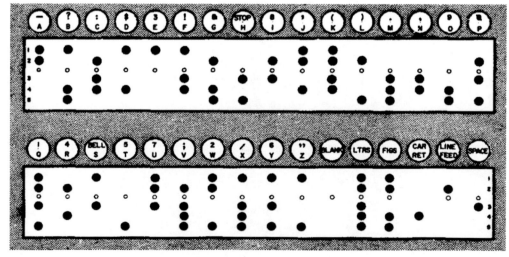

Murray's most important innovation was to record the bit combinations as holes punched into paper tape. This allowed the messages to prerecorded, and then fed one after another at high speed into an automated reader, making better use of the telegraph line. Additionally, as the tape system solved the issue of operator fatigue, the coding was chosen so as minimize wear on the equipment rather than for typing convenience.

Paper tape containing Murray code:

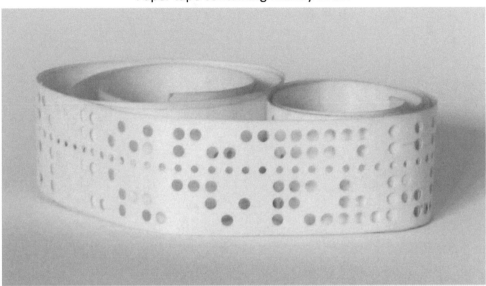

ASCII

By the early 1960s, improvements in technology meant that using more than five bits in a teleprinter code was becoming an affordable option. There was also a demand for more sophisticated data transmission, such as allowing lowercase characters, more symbols, and more characters. This led to the development of the 7-bit **American Standard Code for Information Interchange** (ASCII pronounced "as-key") in 1964. Although developed with telegraphy in mind, ASCII also incorporated features designed to assist with automated data processing (for example when using a computer), such as choosing codes that would be easy to alphabetically sort, and which could easily be converted between upper and lower case.

ASCII character set:

(control characters are shown with a pink background)

NUL	SOH	STX	ETX	EOT	ENQ	ACK	BEL	BS	HT	LF	VT	FF	CR	SO	SI
DLE	DC1	DC2	DC3	DC4	NAK	SYN	ETB	CAN	EM	SUB	ESC	FS	GS	RS	US
	!	"	#	$	%	&	'	(	)	*	+	,	-	.	/
0	1	2	3	4	5	6	7	8	9	:	;	<	=	>	?
@	A	B	C	D	E	F	G	H	I	J	K	L	M	N	O
P	Q	R	S	T	U	V	W	X	Y	Z	[	\	]	^	_
`	a	b	c	d	e	f	g	h	i	j	k	l	m	n	o
p	q	r	s	t	u	v	w	x	y	z	{	|	}	~	DEL

Computer Codes

Computers internally store and process information as binary numbers. A binary number consists of a series of 1s and 0s each of which is represented internally by the on/off statuses of a switch or electric current through a circuit. As with the Baudot code, each binary digit is called a bit.

This memory chip from a video game console stores over 16,000 bits of information:

A typical computer contains thousands, millions or even billions of bits of storage. To allow computers to represent text and other human-readable information, various codes have been devised which describe how the text and other human-readable information can be encoded into a series of on/off bits. This topic is discussed in much more detail in chapters 3, 8, 9, 11, 12 and 13 of my book Advanced Binary for Programming & Computer Science: Logical, Bitwise and Arithmetic Operations, and Data Encoding and Representation, but we can briefly touch on some key points here:

- There are many types of computer codes for representing different types of data such as unsigned (non-negative) whole numbers (integers), signed (positive or negative) integers, decimals, fractions, graphics and text.
- Even for the same type of data, there are many possible coding schemes that could potentially be used. Different types of computer, and sometimes different software on the same computer, may use different codes to represent the same type of data.
- There can be advantages and disadvantages to using different codes. Different codes can vary in the amount of storage used, the ease of data processing, and in the range of characters, numbers or other data that they are able to represent.

As far as characters and textual data is concerned:

- The most popular early standard for representing characters was the ASCII standard, which was inherited from electrical telegraphy. ASCII is a 7-bit per character system and supports 128 different characters of which, 33 are control code characters, 94 are printable characters, and 1 is the space character. The printable characters include both uppercase and lowercase English letters, numeric digits, punctuation marks and symbols, as well as some common mathematical and typographic symbols.

- Many computers have been designed around the idea of dividing storage and data communication into units of 8 bits (known as **bytes**). It was therefore natural on such computers to store one ASCII character per byte, even though this left one bit unused in each byte. Rather than waste this bit, many computer manufacturers took advantage of this spare bit to produce their own extended variants of ASCII which added additional character codes for accented or Greek letters, graphical symbols, and/or additional mathematical symbols.
- Although ASCII and variants of ASCII were the most common early codes used for storing textual data, there were also many different proprietary coding systems. Most of these are now virtually forgotten today and only of historical interest, but an IBM coding system called **Extended Binary Coded Decimal Interchange Code (EBCDIC)** did become widespread.
- As computers grew in power and storage capabilities, demand grew for a coding system with codes for foreign language alphabets such as Hebrew, Arabic, Japanese and Chinese, emojis, more mathematical and typographic symbols and so on. This led to the development of the **Unicode** standard, which is still growing, but as of May 2019 provides codes for almost 138,000 different characters.
- Today, ASCII, EBCDIC and Unicode all remain in widespread use.

Printable characters included into the IBM PC's built-in extended version of ASCII:

(today known as **Code page 437**, **CP437**, **OEM-US**, **OEM 437**, **PC-8**, or **DOS Latin US**)

Chapter 2: Caesar Ciphers

The **Caesar cipher** (also known as **Caesar's cipher**, **Caesar's code**, **Caesar's shift** or a **shift cipher**) is one of the simplest and earliest-known methods of enciphering a message. It is named after Julius Caesar (July 12th or 13th, 100 BC to March 15th, 44BC) who is known to have used this type of cipher.

Bust of Julius Caesar:

Using a Caesar Cipher

To encipher a message into a Caesar cipher, each letter of the plaintext is shifted forward or backward through the alphabet by a chosen number of places. Julius Caesar himself is said to have used a forward shift of 3 places, with "A" being enciphered to "D", "B" to "E", "C" to "F", and so on.

In the case of letters near the end or beginning of the alphabet, you simply loop round if necessary. So, with a forward shift of 3 places, "X" would be enciphered to "A", "Y" to "B", and "Z" to "C".

Enciphering into a Caesar cipher with a forward shift of 3 characters:

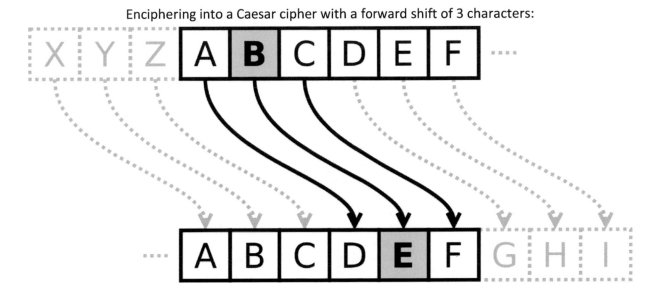

To decipher a message in a Caesar cipher, simply shift the letters in the ciphertext in the opposite direction by the same number of places. For example, if a forward shift of 3 places is used when enciphering, a backward shift of 3 places would be used when deciphering. As with enciphering, when deciphering, for some letters, it may be necessary to loop round the alphabet.

Deciphering from a Caesar cipher with a backward shift of 3 characters:

Variations of the Caesar Cipher

There are some variations possible in a Caesar cipher:

- There is the choice of shift to be used when enciphering. Using the standard English alphabet there are 25 possible shifts (a shift backwards of 1 place is equivalent to a forward shift of 25, a shift backwards of 2 places is equivalent to a forward shift of 24, and so on).
- We could use an extended alphabet containing additional symbols such as "ABCDEFGHIJKLMNOPQRSTUVWXYZ0123456789". In this case, a forward shift of 5 places would result in "Z" be enciphered as "4", "Y" as "3", and so on.
- In cases, where the shift results in reaching past the end of the alphabet, instead of looping round, we could substitute a special character or characters. Julius Caesar's nephew Augustus (September 23rd, 63 BC to August 19th, 14 AD), who went on to become the first Roman Emperor, is said to have done exactly that: Augustus used a forward shift of 1 place with "Z" enciphered as "AA".

Statue of Augustus:

ROT13

ROT13 (also known as **ROT-13** or **rotate by 13 places**) is an example of a Caesar cipher that is still widely used today, albeit only for messages where security is **not** a concern and it does **not** matter if they are easily deciphered by anybody. For example, ROT13 is often used to hide punchlines to jokes or solutions to puzzles.

ROT13 uses only the uppercase letters of the English alphabet. To encipher a message into ROT13, simply shift the letters forward through the alphabet by 13 places (it does **not** matter whether you consider this a 13-place forward or 13-place backward shift since both result in the same ciphertext).

To decipher a message from ROT13, you also simply shift the letters by 13 places (again it does **not** matter whether you consider this a 13-place forward or 13-place backward shift since both result in the same plaintext).

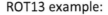

ROT13 example:

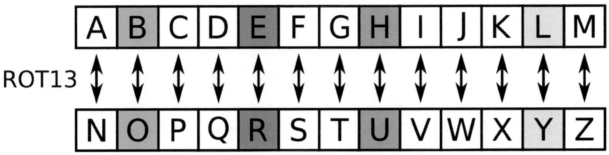

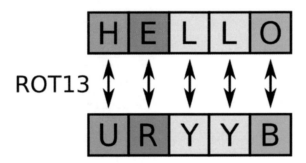

Since the exact same shifting process can be used for enciphering and deciphering, ROT13 is its own inverse (**symmetric** or **self-reciprocal**). Performing ROT13 twice on the same piece of text, takes you back to where you started, since the first ROT13 enciphers the text and second ROT13 deciphers it.

ROT5

A similar algorithm to ROT13, known as **ROT5** (or **ROT-5**), can be used for numeric digits. In ROT5 we cycle each digit by 5 places (looping round if necessary), so "0" is enciphered as "5", "1" as "6", "2" as "7", and so on. Like ROT13, ROT5 is its own inverse, so to decipher ciphertext that was enciphered with ROT5, simply perform ROT5 on it.

ROT18

Since ROT13 enciphers only letters, and ROT5 enciphers only digits, if we have a message containing both letters and digits, an obvious method of enciphering the entire message is to use ROT13 on the letters and ROT5 on the digits. This is known as **ROT18** (or **ROT-18** or **ROT13.5** or **ROT-13.5**), and like ROT13 and ROT5 is its own inverse.

ROT47

Another variant based on using a different alphabet is ROT47 (or ROT-47). This method uses an extended alphabet with 94 different characters and a shift of 47 places through that alphabet. The extended alphabet consists of all the printable characters in the ASCII character set used by many computers (see Chapter 1) and contains letters (uppercase and lowercase letters are treated as separate), numeric digits, and common punctuation and mathematical symbols. As with ROT13, ROT5 and ROT18, ROT47 is self-reciprocal.

Avgad and Albam

According to Kabbalahists (a school of Jewish mysticism), there are hidden meanings enciphered within the Hebrew text of the Bible. Kabbalahists claim there are several different ciphers used (most of which are beyond the scope of this book), but two of them are types of Caesar ciphers:

- Avgad – In **Avgad**, the hidden meanings can be revealed by replacing each letter with the previous letter of the alphabet (so the message was enciphered by a forward shift of 1 character).
- Albam – In **Albam**, the hidden meanings can be revealed by shifting each letter by 11 characters forward through the alphabet (so the message was enciphered by a forward shift of 11 characters).

If you were to perform Avgad or Albam on English text, the result would most likely to be unpronounceable nonsense. However, because of the different structure of written Hebrew from written English, using Avgad or Albam on Hebrew often results readable or apparently meaningful results.

Breaking Caesar Ciphers

A Caesar cipher using just the standard alphabet can **always** be easily broken – simply try all 25 possible shifts (trying every combination is known as **brute force attack**). In fact, in many cases it is **not** even necessary to try all possible shifts: the most common letter in all but the shortest English texts is nearly always "E", so simply try the shift that restores deciphers the most common letter in the ciphertext back into an "E".

Here is an example of deciphering a cryptogram in a Caesar cipher back into plaintext:

- Cryptogram: "GKXJFIDFYRNISNLMY"
- Backward shift of 1 place results in "FJWIEHCEXQMHRMKLX". Keep trying...
- Backward shift of 2 places results in "EHUHDGBDWPLGQLJKW". Keep trying...

- Backward shift of 3 places results in "DGTGCFACVOKFPKIJV". Keep trying...
- Backward shift of 4 places results in "CFSFBEZBUNJEOJHIU". Keep trying...
- Backward shift of 5 places results in "BEREADYATMIDNIGHT". We've found it! Adding spaces, the plaintext reads "BE READY AT MIDNIGHT".

What about messages in a Caesar cipher in an extended alphabet? In this case, we could try and guess what the extended alphabet contains and the order of the characters within it, but if this fails we are **not** lost: we can use frequency analysis (see Chapter 3) as we would with any other substitution code.

Chapter 3: Simple Substitution Ciphers

In a simple substitution cipher, each letter (or character or symbol) in a plaintext message is enciphered into a different letter (or character or symbol) in the ciphertext version of the message. The same substitution is always used for each occurrence of a letter (or character or symbol) in the plaintext message. For example, if the first occurrence plaintext character "A" is enciphered to "B", then all subsequent occurrences of "A" in the plaintext are also enciphered to "B".

Atbash Cipher

Atbash is the name of a cipher known since ancient times and used at places within the Bible. In the Atbash cipher, the first letter of the alphabet is enciphered as the last letter of the alphabet ("A" would be enciphered to "Z" in English), the second letter of the alphabet is enciphered as the last letter of the alphabet ("B" would be enciphered to "Y" in English), and so on. In the Bible, Atbash was performed using the Hebrew alphabet, and its name reflects that fact: it is named for the first, last, second and second to last letters of the Hebrew alphabet (Aleph, Taw, Bet, Shin).

How to use the Atbash cipher with English:

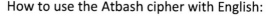
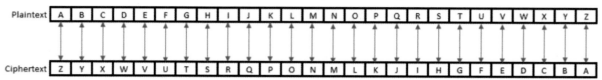

Because of the different structure of written Hebrew from written English, whereas English words enciphered using Atbash would end-up as nonsense, Hebrew words would usually encipher into readable results. Some claimed examples of Atbash are found in Bible verses including Jeremiah 25:26 and 51:41 (which both refer to "Sheshach" which is Atbash for Babylon), and Jeremiah 51:1 (which refers to "Leb Kamai" which is Atbash for Chaldea).

It should be noted that while Atbash provides a simple method of enciphering text, it provides absolutely no security against an attacker who is aware of the algorithm. Text in Atbash ciphertext can be trivially deciphered by anybody.

Example:

- The plaintext "SECRET MESSAGE" would encipher using Atbash to "HVXIV GNVHH ZTV" (spaces are skipped when enciphering, and ciphertext letters arranged into groups of five).
- The ciphertext "YVKIV KZIVW" would decipher to "BEPRE PARED" which of course is intended to be read as "BE PREPARED".

Simple Alphabetic Substitution Ciphers

In an **alphabetic substitution cipher**, each plaintext character potentially be enciphered into **any** ciphertext character. The relationship between plaintext and ciphertext can be entirely arbitrary: for example, "A" in plaintext might be enciphered to "B", "B" in plaintext to "M", "C" to "F", "D" to "A", and so on.

Example of a simple alphabetic substitution cipher:

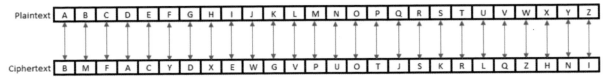

As there is no simple rule for enciphering and deciphering each character, there are a vast number of possible ways of enciphering a message. For example, if we restrict ourselves to the 26 uppercase letters of the English alphabet, there are over 400,000,000,000,000,000,000,000,000 possible ways to encipher a message using a simple alphabetic substitution cipher. The vast number of permutations means that even using a computer, it is **not** possible for an attacker to perform a brute force attack on an enciphered message by trying to decipher it using every possible combination.

It should also be noted that the Caesar ciphers that we discussed in Chapter 2 can be regarded as a special case of a simple alphabetic substitution cipher. Of course, the weakness of Caesar ciphers is that the same rule is applied to all characters during the enciphering process, which drastically reduces the number of possible permutations and makes a brute force attack feasible. As we've noted already, using the 26 characters of the English alphabet, there are only 25 ways to encipher a message using a Caesar cipher, as opposed to over 400,000,000,000,000,000,000,000,000 ways using a simple alphabetic substitution cipher.

Examples:

- If we wanted to encipher the message "BEWARE THE IDES OF MARCH" using the simple alphabetic substitution cipher shown above: "B" would be enciphered to "M", "E" to "C", "W" to "Z", and so on. The entire message enciphered (removing spaces and arranging characters into groups of five) would read "MCZBS CRXCE ACKOY PRSFX".
- Likewise, if received the enciphered message "VOOGM CXEUA NOL" using the same simple alphabetic substitution cipher: "V" would be deciphered to "L", "O" to "O", "G" to "K", and so on. The entire deciphered message would read "LOOKB EHIND YOU", which rearranging to put spaces in the correct places gives "LOOK BEHIND YOU".

Simple Symbolic Substitution Ciphers

In a simple symbolic substitution cipher, each letter (or character or symbol) in the plaintext message, instead of being enciphered into a letter, is enciphered into a different symbol in the ciphertext version of the message. The same symbol is always used for each occurrence of a letter (or character or symbol) in the plaintext message.

Pigpen Cipher

The **Pigpen cipher** (also known as the **masonic cipher, Freemason's cipher, Napoleon cipher** and **tic-tac-toe cipher**) is one of the best-known simple symbolic substitution ciphers. In Pigpen each letter is encoded as a combination of horizontal, vertical and diagonal lines, possibly accompanied by a dot.

To encipher a letter using Pigpen, we use the Pigpen cipher key (shown below). Look at the lines adjacent to the letter on the cipher key, and these lines are used to indicate the letter, adding a dot if there is a dot in the corresponding space on the cipher key.

Pigpen cipher key:

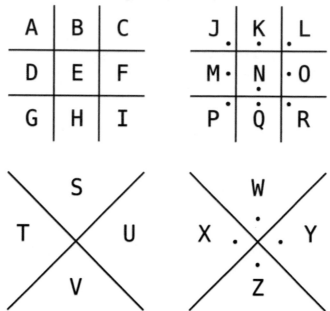

For example:

- If we wanted to encipher the letter "H", we would see that the cipher key contains vertical lines to the left and right of the letter as well as a horizontal line above it. This shape: ⊓. Hence the letter "H" is enciphered as ⊓.
- If we wanted to encipher the letter "T", we would see that the cipher key has diagonals lines above and below the letter. This shape: >. Hence the letter "T" is enciphered as >.
- If we wanted to encipher the letter "P", we would see that the cipher key has a vertical line to the right of the letter, a horizontal line above it, and a dot next to it. This shape: •⌐. Hence the letter "P" is enciphered as •⌐.

To decipher a message in Pigpen, we simply reverse the process, locating the corresponding letter based on the symbol. Here is an example of decoding a secret message written in the Pigpen cipher:

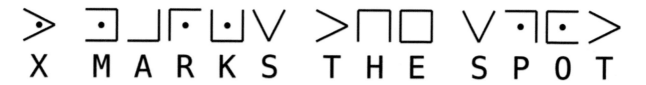

An obvious weakness of the Pigpen cipher is that once an attacker has seen the cipher key, it is trivial for them to decipher any message. One way to make this more difficult and maintain a degree of secrecy is to rearrange the letters on the cipher key in an agreed manner. That way, only people who seen the modified cipher key can easily decipher the message.

As well as rearranging the letters on the grids, other variants of the Pigpen cipher can be obtained by using different shape or design grids. Some well-known variants include:

- The **Rosicrucian cipher** – This uses a grid with nine cells. The top left cell contains "ABC", the top middle cell contains "DEF" and so on. Each letter is enciphered by as the lines adjacent to that letter's cell plus 1, 2 or 3 dots to indicate the letter's position within that cell.
- The **Newark cipher** – This uses letters placed on a grid and the lines adjacent to each letter's cell, but instead of using dots to distinguish otherwise identical cells, 1, 2 or 3 short lines are added. The short lines, which can be drawn at any angle or orientation, are intended to give the impression that there are many more than 26 different symbols.
- The **Templar cipher** – This cipher was allegedly used by the Knights Templar and uses a design based on the Maltese Cross to encipher each letter.

Symbols in the Templar cipher:

No variant of the Pigpen cipher is secure against a determined attacker. All these variants are well-known, but even for a new variant (such as rearranging the letters), an attacker can use some relatively simple techniques (like Frequency Analysis – see below) to break the cipher.

Breaking Simple Substitution Ciphers

Although simple alphabetic substitution and simple symbolic substitution ciphers allow messages to be enciphered in a vast number of different ways, they can usually be deciphered by an attacker relatively easily. Most cryptograms can be deciphered with a few hours work using pen and paper, or almost instantly using a computer (there are software and websites that can do this task).

Frequency Analysis

If you play the boardgame *Scrabble*, you will notice that there are a lot more tiles with the letter "E" than any other letter: there are 12 "E" tiles in English language Scrabble sets. Similarly, there are 6 "N" tiles in English language sets, but only 2 "V" tiles, and only 1 "J" tile. This intended to reflect the fact that in written English, some letters in are much more commonly used than others.

If we look at any piece of written English text (unless it is very short or unusually written), some facts are almost always true:

- The most common letter in written English is "E". So, for any cryptogram, it is also likely that the most common letter will be "E". It is therefore likely that the most common (or one of the most common) letters in the ciphertext deciphers to "E".

- The second most common letter in English is "T". So, it is likely that one of the most common letters in the ciphertext deciphers to "T".
- Third most common letter in English is "A". So, it is likely that one of the most common letters in the ciphertext deciphers to "A".
- The next nine most common letters in English (in order from highest to lowest frequency) are in fact "O", "I", "N", "S", "H", "R", "D", "L" and "U". So, it is likely that some of the most common letters in the ciphertext decipher to these letters.
- Some two-letter combinations of letters (**bigrams** or **digrams**) such as "EE", "OO" and "TT" occur commonly in written English, but other combinations such as "AA" and "II" are very rare. The twenty most common bigrams in English (in order from most to least common) are "TH", "HE", "IN", "ER", "AN", "RE", "ES", "ST", "ON", "ND", "EN", "AT", "NT", "ED", "EA", "TO", "OR", "TI", "HA" and "AR". It is likely that the most common bigrams in the ciphertext will correspond to the most common bigrams in English.

Relative frequencies of letters in typical English text:

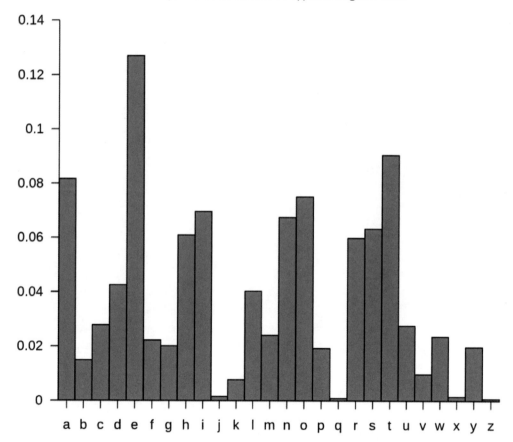

We can use these facts to help us decipher almost any message enciphered using a simple substitution cipher, even if we do **not** know how it was enciphered. For example, can make an educated guess than the most common letter in the cryptogram is an enciphered "E", "T" or "A", and the most common bigrams are "TH", "HE", "IN" or "ER". This technique of using the relative frequencies of different letters and groups of letters to break a cipher is known as **frequency analysis**.

EXAMPLE:

Can we decipher the following cryptogram (spaces and punctuation have been removed):
"QSHIQZTQDZGQZZQEAQZRQVFWTZQZTQDZGLTEXKTYSQFALUQDDQZTQDZGHKGCORTEGCTKOFUY
OKTDOLLOGFGWPTEZOCTLDXLZWTQEIOTCTRKTUQKRSTLLGYEGLZQEZOGFZIOLRQN"

Counting the number of appearances of each letter, the six most common letters are:
- "Q" which occurs 17 times.
- "T" which occurs 16 times.
- "Z" which occurs 15 times.
- "L" and "G" which each occur 10 times.
- "O" which occurs 9 times.

It is highly likely that these correspond to the most common letters in English, although we can **not** be sure which is which. It is also likely that the ciphertext letters "Q", "T" and "Z" correspond to the plaintext letters "A", "E" and "T", although again we can **not** be sure which is which.

The eleven most common bigrams in the ciphertext are:
- "QZ" which occurs 5 times.
- "QD" and "TQ" which occurs 4 times.
- "KT", "ZT", "ZG", "TE", "ZQ", "QE", "CT" and "DZ", which each occur 3 times.

As we decipher the cryptogram, I will show our progress as shown below in Figure 1. The red letters are the ciphertext, the black letters show the deciphered plaintext message (initially no letters have been deciphered so all are "?"s).

Figure 1:

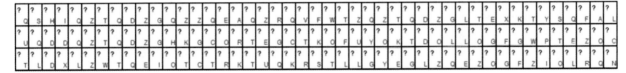

FIRST GUESS:

If we guess the "Q" is the ciphertext for plaintext "E", "T" is the ciphertext for plaintext "A", and "Z" is the ciphertext for plaintext "T", then this would mean the cryptogram would decipher:

Figure 2:

According to this guess, the common ciphertext bigrams would decipher (using "?" for unknown characters):
- Ciphertext "QZ" would correspond to plaintext "ET".

- Ciphertext "TQ" would correspond to plaintext "AE", ciphertext "ZQ" would correspond to plaintext "TE", ciphertext "QD" would correspond to plaintext "E?", ciphertext "KT" would correspond to plaintext "?A", and so on.
- It seems quite unlikely that "AE", a very uncommon bigram in English, should occur four times within the same short message, even if some of these span words so that "A" ends one word and "E" begins the next word.
- Furthermore, if we look at the deciphered text Figure 2, it includes an odd-looking sequence of letters: "ATEETAE". Wherever we put wordbreaks, this sequence probably would **not** appear in any English language text.
- So, for the time being, let us reject this guess (we can always return to it later if other approaches do **not** work out).

SECOND GUESS:

If we guess the "Q" is the ciphertext for plaintext "E", "T" is the ciphertext for plaintext "T", and "Z" is the ciphertext for plaintext "A", then this would mean the cryptogram would decipher:

Figure 3:

- Ciphertext "QZ" would correspond to plaintext "EA" .
- Ciphertext "TQ" would correspond to plaintext "TE", ciphertext "ZQ" would correspond to plaintext "AE", ciphertext "QD" would correspond to plaintext "E?", ciphertext "KT" would correspond to plaintext "?T", and so on.
- Again, it seems unlikely that "AE", a very uncommon bigram in English, should occur four times within the same short message, even if some of these span words so that "A" ends one word and "E" begins the next word.
- Furthermore, if we look at the deciphered text Figure 3, it includes some odd-looking sequences of letters: "EAAE" and "TAEATE". Wherever we put wordbreaks, these sequences probably would **not** appear in any English language text.
- So, for the time being, let us reject this guess (we can always return to it later if other approaches do **not** work out).

THIRD GUESS:

If we guess the "Q" is the ciphertext for plaintext "A", "T" is the ciphertext for plaintext "E", and "Z" is the ciphertext for plaintext "T", then this would mean the cryptogram would decipher:

Figure 4:

- Ciphertext "QZ" would correspond to plaintext "AT" .

- Ciphertext "TQ" would correspond to plaintext "EA", ciphertext "ZQ" would correspond to plaintext "TA", ciphertext "QD" would correspond to plaintext "A?", ciphertext "KT" would correspond to plaintext "?E", and so on.
- There are no repeated rare bigrams such as the "AE"s of the first and second guesses.
- Looking at the deciphered text in Figure 4, there are no sequences that appear obviously impossible. The only sequence that might be of concern is "ETATEA", but we could imagine wordbreaks giving "…ET A TEA…" or "…ETA TEA…" which would be plausible text.
- So, for now, let assume that our that our guess about the three most common characters is correct.

REFINING THE THIRD GUESS

We now beginning looking in at the next common characters in the ciphertext:

- The three next most common letters in the ciphertext are "L", "G" and "O". Each of these probably corresponds to a different one of the next most common letters in English: "O", "I", "N", "S", "H", "R", "D", "L" and "U". Obviously, the difficulty is figuring out which is which.
- Looking at the ciphertext, there are 2 occurrences of "LL". As "II", "HH" and "UU" are uncommon in English (even when these letters end one word and start the next), we can guess that the ciphertext character "L" probably corresponds to plaintext "O", "N", "S", "R", "D" or "L".
- In the ciphertext, we also notice the strings of characters "OLLOG", "TLLG" and "GLZQ".
- If ciphertext "L" were plaintext "O", these strings would decipher to "?OO??", "EOO" and "?OTA". "EOO" does **not** seem to be a likely letter combination in English, so we can conclude that ciphertext "L" is probably **not** plaintext "O".
- What if ciphertext "L" corresponded to plaintext "N"? In this case, the ciphertext strings would correspond to the plaintext strings "?NN??", "ENN?" and "?NTA". This seems possible. If it is correct, it is also likely that the first two "?"s in "?NN??" are vowels, and because they are both "O" in ciphertext, they must both be the same vowel in the plaintext. This vowel can **not** be "A" or "E" as they have already been used in the plaintext, so must "I", "O" or "U". So ciphertext "O" must correspond to plaintext "I", "O" or "U". Likewise, the "?" in "?NTA" is highly likely to be a vowel, so ciphertext "G" must also be "I", "O" or "U". If we try all combinations, this is how the entire message would decipher:

Figure 5:

Ciphertext L corresponds to	Ciphertext G corresponds to	Ciphertext O corresponds to	Entire cryptogram deciphered
N	I	O	A???ATEA?TIATTA??AT?A???ETATEA?TINE???E??A??N?A??ATEA?TI??I?O?E?I?E?O ???O?E?ONNOI?I??E?TO?EN??NT?EA??OE?E??E?A???ENNI??INTA?TOI?T?ON?A?
N	I	U	A???ATEA?TIATTA??AT?A???ETATEA?TINE???E??A??N?A??ATEA?TI??I?U?E?I?E?U ???U?E?UNNUI?I??E?TU?EN??NT?EA??UE?E??E?A???ENNI??INTA?TUI?T?UN?A?
N	O	I	A???ATEA?TOATTA??AT?A???ETATEA?TONE???E??A??N?A??ATEA?TO??O?I?E?O?E?I ???I?E?INNIO?O??E?TI?EN??NT?EA??IE?E??E?A???ENNO??ONTA?TIO?T?IN?A?
N	O	U	A???ATEA?TOATTA??AT?A???ETATEA?TONE???E??A??N?A??ATEA?TO??O?U?E?O?E?U ???U?E?UNNUO?O??E?TU?EN??NT?EA??UE?E??E?A???ENNO??ONTA?TUO?T?UN?A?
N	U	I	A???ATEA?TUATTA??AT?A???ETATEA?TUNE???E??A??N?A??ATEA?TU??U?I?E?U?E?I ???I?E?INNIU?U??E?TI?EN??NT?EA??IE?E??E?A???ENNU??UNTA?TIU?T?IN?A?
N	U	O	A???ATEA?TUATTA??AT?A???ETATEA?TUNE???E??A??N?A??ATEA?TU??U?O?E?U?E?O ???O?E?ONNUO?U??E?TO?EN??NT?EA??OE?E??E?A???ENNU??UNTA?TOU?T?ON?A?

- Looking more closely at Figure 5, we notice that every combination generates some unlikely looking strings in the plaintext (which are highlighted in red below):

Figure 6:

Ciphertext L corresponds to	Ciphertext G corresponds to	Ciphertext O corresponds to	**Entire cryptogram deciphered**
N	I	O	A???ATEA TIATTA ??AT?A???ETATEA?TINE???E??A??N?A??ATEA?TI??I?O?E?I?E?O ???O?E? ONNOI ?I??E?TO?EN??NT?EA??OE?E??E?A???ENNI??INTA?TOI?T?ON?A?
N	I	U	A???ATEA TIATTA ?AT?A???ETATEA?TINE???E??A??N?A??ATEA?TI??I?U?E?I?E?U ???U?E? UNNUI ?I??E?TU?EN??NT?EA??UE?E??E?A???ENNI??INTA?TUI?T?UN?A?
N	O	I	A???ATEA?TOATTA??AT?A???ETATEA?TONE???E??A??N?A??ATEA?TO??O?I?E?O?E?I ???I?E? INNIO ?O??E?TI?EN??NT?EA??IE?E??E?A???ENNO??ONTA?TIO?T?IN?A?
N	O	U	A???ATEA?TOATTA??AT?A???ETATEA?TONE???E??A??N?A??ATEA?TO??O?U?E?O?E?U ???U?E? UNNUO ?O??E?TU?EN??NT?EA??UE?E??E?A???ENNO??ONTA?TUO?T?UN?A?
N	U	I	A???ATEA TUATTA ?AT?A???ETATEA?TUNE???E??A??N?A??ATEA?TU??U?I?E?U?E?I ???I?E?INNIU?U??E?TI?EN??NT?EA??IE?E??E?A???ENNU??UNTA?TIU?T?IN?A?
N	U	O	A???ATEA? TUATTA ??AT?A???ETATEA?TUNE???E??A??N?A??ATEA?TU??U?O?E?U?E?O ???O?E? ONNOU ?U??E?TO?EN??NT?EA??OE?E??E?A???ENNU??UNTA?TOU?T?ON?A?

- We seem to have reached a dead-end, so we need to backtrack. The most recent guess that we made was that ciphertext "L" corresponded to plaintext "N" – we then followed the logical implications of that, and it led to a dead-end. So, it seems that ciphertext "L" can **not** correspond to plaintext "N". It must correspond to a different character. The other likely options we have are "S", "R", "D" or "L", so let's assume that ciphertext "L" corresponds to plaintext "S".

- If ciphertext "L" does represent plaintext "S", the ciphertext strings "OLLOG", "TLLG" and "GLZQ" would correspond to the plaintext strings "?SS??", "ESS?" and "?STA". This seems possible. If it is correct, it is also likely that the first two "?"s in "?SS??" are vowels, and because they are both "O" in ciphertext, they must both be the same vowel in the plaintext. This vowel can **not** be "A" or "E" as they have already been used in the plaintext, so must "I", "O" or "U". So ciphertext "O" must correspond to plaintext "I", "O" or "U". Likewise, the "?" in "?STA" is highly likely to be a vowel, so ciphertext "G" must also be "I", "O" or "U". If we try all combinations, this is how the entire message would decipher:

Figure 7:

Ciphertext L corresponds to	Ciphertext G corresponds to	Ciphertext O corresponds to	**Entire cryptogram deciphered**
S	I	O	A???ATEA?TIATTA??AT?A???ETATEA?TISE???E??A??S?A??ATEA?TI??I?O?E?I?E?O ???O?E?OSSOI?I??E?TO?ES??ST?EA??OE?E??E?A???ESSI??ISTA?TOI?T?OS?A?
S	I	U	A???ATEA?TIATTA??AT?A???ETATEA?TISE???E??A??S?A??ATEA?TI??I?U?E?I?E?U ???U?E?USSUI?I??E?TU?ES??ST?EA??UE?E??E?A???ESSI??ISTA?TUI?T?US?A?
S	O	I	A???ATEA?TOATTA??AT?A???ETATEA?TOSE???E??A??S?A??ATEA?TO??O?I?E?O?E?I ???I?E?ISSIO?O??E?TI?ES??ST?EA??IE?E??E?A???ESSO??OSTA?TIO?T?IS?A?
S	O	U	A???ATEA?TOATTA??AT?A???ETATEA?TOSE???E??A??S?A??ATEA?TO??O?U?E?O?E?U ???U?E?USSUO?O??E?TU?ES??ST?EA??UE?E??E?A???ESSO??OSTA?TUO?T?US?A?
S	U	I	A???ATEA?TUATTA??AT?A???ETATEA?TUSE???E??A??S?A??ATEA?TU??U?I?E?U?E?I ???I?E?ISSIU?U??E?TI?ES??ST?EA??IE?E??E?A???ESSU??USTA?TIU?T?IS?A?
S	U	O	A???ATEA?TUATTA??AT?A???ETATEA?TUSE???E??A??S?A??ATEA?TU??U?O?E?U?E?O ???O?E?OSSOU?U??E?TO?ES??ST?EA??OE?E??E?A???ESSU??USTA?TOU?T?OS?A?

- Looking closely at Figure 7, we can see that most combinations generate some unlikely looking strings in the plaintext (which are highlighted in red below), but one version contains some plausible strings at the same positions (which are highlighted in blue):

Figure 8:

Ciphertext L corresponds to	Ciphertext G corresponds to	Ciphertext O corresponds to	Entire cryptogram deciphered
S	I	O	A???ATEA?TIATTA??AT?A???ETATEA?TISE???E??A??S?A??ATEA?TI??I?O?E?I?E?O ???O?E?OSSO?I??E?TO?ES??ST?EA??OE?E??E?A???ESSI??ISTA?TOI?T?OS?A?
S	I	U	A???ATEA?TIATTA??AT?A???ETATEA?TISE???E??A??S?A??ATEA?TI??I?U?E?I?E?U ???U?E?USSU?I??E?TU?ES??ST?EA??UE?E??E?A???ESSI??ISTA?TUI?T?US?A?
S	O	I	A???ATEA?TOATTA??AT?A???ETATEA?TOSE???E??A??S?A??ATEA?TO??O?I?E?O?E?I ???I?E?ISSIO?O??E?TI?ES??ST?EA??IE?E??E?A???ESSO??OSTA?TIO?T?IS?A?
S	O	U	A???ATEA?TOATTA??AT?A???ETATEA?TOSE???E??A??S?A??ATEA?TO??O?U?E?O?E?U ???U?E?USSUO?O??E?TU?ES??ST?EA??UE?E??E?A???ESSO??OSTA?TUO?T?US?A?
S	U	I	A???ATEA?TUATTA??AT?A???ETATEA?TUSE???E??A??S?A??ATEA?TU??I?U?E?U?E?I ???I?E?ISSIU?U??E?TI?ES??ST?EA??IE?E??E?A???ESSU??USTA?TIU?T?IS?A?
S	U	O	A???ATEA?TUATTA??AT?A???ETATEA?TUSE???E??A??S?A??ATEA?TU??U?O?E?U?E?O ???O?E?OSSOU?U??E?TO?ES??ST?EA??OE?E??E?A???ESSU??USTA?TOU?T?OS?A?

- The blue highlighted strings might be parts of phrases like "TO ATTACK" or "TO ATTACH", and "MISSION" or "FISSION", respectively.
- The ciphertext character that corresponds to the first "?" after "TOATTA" is "E". Let us for now assume that ciphertext "E" corresponds to plaintext "C".
- The ciphertext character that corresponds to the first "?" after "ISSIO" is "F". Let us for now assume that ciphertext "F" corresponds to plaintext "N".
- We now have hypothesized that ciphertext "Q", "T" and "Z" correspond to plaintext "A", "E" and "T". That ciphertext "L", "G" and "O" correspond to plaintext "S", "O" and "I". And that that ciphertext "E" and "F" correspond to plaintext "C" and "N". If we try to decipher the entire cryptogram according to these rules, we almost have a recognizable message:

Figure 9:

- Looking at the last few characters, we can probably guess that the sequence "ACTIONT?IS?A?" probably is meant to decipher to "ACTION THIS DAY". The "?"s in this string correspond to the ciphertext characters "I", "R" and "N", which would correspond to the plaintext "H", "D" and "Y". In this case, the entire cryptogram would now decipher:

Figure 10:

- We can now go back and have a look at "TOATTAC?". Since we already have already found the ciphertext character "I" corresponds to the plaintext character "H", there can **not** be another ciphertext character that also corresponds to the plaintext character "H". So, "TOATTAC?" must be meant to be "TO ATTACK" rather than "TO ATTACH". This tells us that the ciphertext character "A" corresponds to the plaintext character "K".
- Using that information and deciphering the entire cryptogram yields:

Figure 11:

- Looking the plaintext "O?COST" near the end, we might guess this is meant to read "ON COST", "OR COST" or "OF COST". We have already found the ciphertext character that corresponds to plaintext "N", so it can **not** be "ON COST". This means the ciphertext character "Y" must correspond to plaintext "R" or "F".
- If we assume that ciphertext "Y" corresponds to plaintext "R" and decipher the whole cryptogram, then we get:

Figure 12:

- On the other hand, if we assume that ciphertext "Y" corresponds to plaintext "F" and decipher the whole cryptogram, then we get:

Figure 13:

- Comparing Figures 12 and 13, it is **not** obvious that one is correct and is incorrect. Since we can **not** tell whether ciphertext "Y" corresponds to plaintext "R" or plaintext "F", let's leave that question unresolved for now. We therefore go back to the situation we were in Figure 11, and try to decipher some other characters instead.

Figure 11 (repeated):

- Looking at the plaintext "A?D?ESS" near the end (middle of third line), we might guess the second "?" (ciphertext "S") corresponds to a plaintext "N", "L" or "R". However, it can **not** be "N" as we have already found the ciphertext character that corresponds to "N". So, it must correspond to plaintext "L" or "R". Trying "L" and deciphering the cryptogram gives:

Figure 14:

- On the other hand, if we were to try "R" instead of "L" and decipher the whole cryptogram, we would get:

Figure 15:

- Now look closely at the beginning of the cryptogram in Figures 14 and 15 (the part that reads "AR?HATEA" or "AL?HATEA". The third character must be one of "B", "D", "F", "G", "J", "M", "P", "Q", "U", "V", "W", "X" "Y" or "Z", or "L" (if the second character is "R"), or "R" (if the second character is "L"), as these are the only plaintext characters that have **not** been used yet. That means the cryptogram must begin "ALBHA", or "ARBHA", or "ALDHA", or "ARDHA", etc. If we work through all the combinations, the only plausible answer is "ALPHA". This means the ciphertext "S" corresponds to plaintext "L", and ciphertext "H" corresponds to plaintext "P".
- Taking advantage of this new information, we can now decipher the entire cryptogram again:

Figure 16:

- Looking at the beginning of the deciphered "ALPHATEA?TOATTACKATDA?N", we can guess the deciphered message probably begins "ALPHA TEAM TO ATTACK AT DAWN". This would mean the ciphertext character "D" corresponds to plaintext "M", and the ciphertext character "V" corresponds to plaintext character "W".
- Taking advantage of this new information, we can decipher the entire cryptogram again:

Figure 17:

A L P H A T E A M T O A T T A C K A T D A W N ? E T A T E A M T O S E C ? ? E F L A N K S
Q S H I Q Z T Q D Z G Q Z Z Q E A Q Z R Q V F W T Z Q Z T Q D Z G L T E X K T Y S Q F A L
? A M M A T E A M T O P ? O ? I D E C O ? E ? I N ? F I ? E M I S S I O N O ? ? E C T I ?
U Q D D Q Z T Q D Z G H K G C O R T E G C T K Q F U Y Q K T D Q L L Q G F G W P T E Z Q C
E S M ? S T ? E A C H I E ? E D ? E ? A ? D L E S S O F C O S T A C T I O N T H I S D A Y
T L D X L Z W T Q E I Q T C T R K T U Q K R S T L L G Y E G L Z Q E Z O G F Z I Q L R Q N

- The next part of the cryptogram begins "?ETATEAMTO", which we can guess probably is intended to read "BETA TEAM TO". This would mean the ciphertext character "W" corresponds to the plaintext character "B".
- Taking advantage of this new information, we can decipher the entire cryptogram again:

Figure 18:

A L P H A T E A M T O A T T A C K A T D A W N B E T A T E A M T O S E C ? ? E F L A N K S
Q S H I Q Z T Q D Z G Q Z Z Q E A Q Z R Q V F W T Z Q Z T Q D Z G L T E X K T Y S Q F A L
? A M M A T E A M T O P ? O ? I D E C O ? E ? I N ? F I ? E M I S S I O N O B ? E C T I ?
U Q D D Q Z T Q D Z G H K G C O R T E G C T K Q F U Y Q K T D Q L L Q G F G W P T E Z Q C
E S M ? S T B E A C H I E ? E D ? E ? A ? D L E S S O F C O S T A C T I O N T H I S D A Y
T L D X L Z W T Q E I Q T C T R K T U Q K R S T L L G Y E G L Z Q E Z O G F Z I Q L R Q N

- We can see the message begins (adding spaces) "ALPHA TEAM TO ATTACK AT DAWN" and continues "BETATEAMTOSEC??E?LANKS" which is probably intended to read "BETA TEAM TO SECURE FLANKS". This would mean the ciphertext characters "X", "K" and "Y" correspond to plaintext characters "U", "R" and "F" respectively.
- Taking advantage of this new information, we can decipher the entire cryptogram again:

Figure 19:

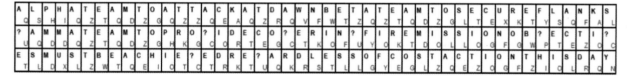

A L P H A T E A M T O A T T A C K A T D A W N B E T A T E A M T O S E C U R E F L A N K S
Q S H I Q Z T Q D Z G Q Z Z Q E A Q Z R Q V F W T Z Q Z T Q D Z G L T E X K T Y S Q F A L
? A M M A T E A M T O P R O ? I D E C O ? E R I N ? F I R E M I S S I O N O B ? E C T I ?
U Q D D Q Z T Q D Z G H K G C O R T E G C T K Q F U Y Q K T D Q L L Q G F G W P T E Z Q C
E S M U S T B E A C H I E ? E D R E ? A R D L E S S O F C O S T A C T I O N T H I S D A Y
T L D X L Z W T Q E I Q T C T R K T U Q K R S T L L G Y E G L Z Q E Z O G F Z I Q L R Q N

- We can probably guess now that the entire cryptogram deciphers to (adding spaces) "ALPHA TEAM TO ATTACK AT DAWN BETA TEAM TO SECURE FLANKS GAMMA TEAM TO PROVIDE COVERING FIRE MISSION OBJECTIVES MUST BE ACHIEVED REGARDLESS OF COST ACTION THIS DAY".

Figure 20:

A L P H A T E A M T O A T T A C K A T D A W N B E T A T E A M T O S E C U R E F L A N K S
Q S H I Q Z T Q D Z G Q Z Z Q E A Q Z R Q V F W T Z Q Z T Q D Z G L T E X K T Y S Q F A L
G A M M A T E A M T O P R O V I D E C O V E R I N G F I R E M I S S I O N O B J E C T I V
U Q D D Q Z T Q D Z G H K G C O R T E G C T K Q F U Y Q K T D Q L L Q G F G W P T E Z Q C
E S M U S T B E A C H I E V E D R E G A R D L E S S O F C O S T A C T I O N T H I S D A Y
T L D X L Z W T Q E I Q T C T R K T U Q K R S T L L G Y E G L Z Q E Z O G F Z I Q L R Q N

- Before assuming that this is correct, we should make sure that we have deciphered the last few characters in a consistent manner (the same ciphertext character should **not** have been deciphered in two different ways). In this case we have: ciphertext character "U" corresponds to plaintext "G", ciphertext "H" to plaintext "P", ciphertext "C" to plaintext "V", and ciphertext "P" to plaintext "J".

- When (or as) we decipher a cryptogram using frequency analysis, we should gradually assemble a cipher key table that records which ciphertext character corresponds to which plaintext character. This key allows us to easily read messages written using the same cipher, and even to create our own enciphered messages.
- Here is the cipher key that we could generate from frequency analysis process in this example. Note that we do **not** know what the ciphertext characters "B", "J" and "M" stand for. They must encode the plaintext characters "Q", "X" and "Z" (since these are the only plaintext characters left), but without further information, it is not possible to tell which of these ciphertext characters to which of these plaintext characters.

Figure 21:

Ciphertext	Plaintext	Ciphertext	Plaintext
A	K	N	Y
B	?	O	I
C	V	P	J
D	M	Q	A
E	C	R	D
F	N	S	L
G	O	T	E
H	P	U	G
I	H	V	W
J	?	W	B
K	R	X	U
L	S	Y	F
M	?	Z	T

Cribs

A crib is some piece of information about the content of the plaintext, which can be used to make cryptanalysis (codebreaking) easier.

For example:

- When deciphering the Enigma code (see Chapter 8), Allied cryptanalysts knew that the plaintext often began "An" (German for "To") and sometimes correctly guessed other words likely to be present in the messages.
- When deciphering the first Zodiac Killer Cipher (see Chapter 14), Bettye Harden correctly guessed that the deciphered text would begin "I" and would also contain "KILL", "KILLING" or "I LIKE KILLING".

To demonstrate the power of cribs, let's take another look at the cryptogram that we previously deciphered using frequency analysis.

Here is how we began:

Figure 1 (repeated):

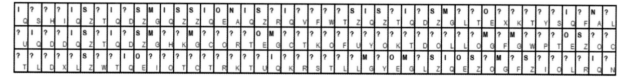

Let us suppose that our is crib is that we know that the plaintext somewhere contains the word "MISSION".

If you look at the word "MISSION", you can see that although seven letters long, it contains only five different letters, that the 2nd and 5th letters are the same as each other, and also that the 3rd and 4th letters are the same as each other Using numbers to identify different letters, we are looking for a pattern of letters that goes "1233245".

Since we are aware that same pattern of letters must occur both in the plaintext and the ciphertext, we look at the ciphertext for that pattern. There are three places where such a pattern occurs:

- In the middle of line 1: "GQZZQEA".
- At the start of line 2: "UQDDQZT".
- In the second half of line 3: "DOLLOGF".

Note: "STLLGYE" in the line 3 is **not** a matching sequence, since its pattern is "1233456".

We then try matching each of "GQZZQEA", "UQDDQZT" and "DOLLOGF" as the crib and see what happens.

- If ciphertext "GQZZQEA" corresponds to plaintext "MISSION", this would mean ciphertext "G" corresponds to plaintext "M", "Q" to "I", "Z" to "S", "E" to "O", and "A" to "N". Deciphering the entire cryptogram on this basis gives:

Figure 22:

- If ciphertext "UQDDQZT" corresponds to plaintext "MISSION", this would mean ciphertext "U" corresponds to plaintext "M", "Q" to "I", "D" to "S", "Z" to "O", and "T" to "N". Deciphering the entire cryptogram on this basis gives:

Figure 23:

- If ciphertext "DOLLOGF" corresponds to plaintext "MISSION", this would mean ciphertext "D" corresponds to plaintext "M", "O" to "I", "L" to "S", "G" to "O", and "F" to "N". Deciphering the entire cryptogram on this basis gives:

Figure 24:

If you look Figures 22, 23 and 24, you will see that Figures 22 and 23 contain some sequences of characters that are unlikely to appear in English text ("SIOS" in Figure 22 and "IOOI" and "NOIONISO" in Figure 23), and so it would be reasonable to conclude that the crib has been used correctly only in Figure 24.

Next, using the same types of frequency analysis we used previously, we can now build on what we already know.

The three most common letters in the ciphertext are:

- "Q" which occurs 17 times.
- "T" which occurs 16 times.
- "Z" which occurs 15 times.

Our crib did **not** tell us how to decipher any of these three letters, but we can guess that they must correspond to plaintext letters "A", "E" and "T" (although we do **not** know which is which).

You may recall that this is similar to the situation that we faced when we tried to decipher the cryptogram using only frequency analysis. This time however, as we can eliminate some options straight away:

- Looking near the beginning of line 2 in Figure 24, we see the ciphertext sequence "QDDQ" which deciphers to "?MM?". It is possible that it is supposed to decipher to "EMME" or "AMMA", but it could **not** be "TMMT". We can conclude that the ciphertext letter "Q" can **not** correspond to plaintext "T", it must correspond to either "E" or "A"
- If we look at the bigrams in the ciphertext, we notice "TQ" and "ZQ" are both very common (4 and 3 occurrences respectively).
- Now if "Q" were the ciphertext for plaintext "E", then "TQ" and "ZQ" must correspond to "AE" and "TE" (although we do **not** know which would be which). It seems implausible that there could be 3 or 4 occurrences of "AE" in such a short message. So, we can conclude that ciphertext "Q" can **not** correspond to plaintext "E".
- On the other hand, if "Q" were the ciphertext for plaintext "A", then "TQ" and "ZQ" must correspond to "EA" and "TA" (again we do **not** know which would be which). It seems highly plausible that there should be 3 or 4 occurrences of these bigrams in the message.
- As we have eliminated all the other likely options for "Q", we can therefore be reasonably confident that ciphertext "Q" corresponds to plaintext "A".
- Taking advantage of this information and deciphering the whole cryptogram yields:

Figure 25:

- We now know that the ciphertext "T" and "Z" must correspond to plaintext "E" and "T", but we still do **not** know which way around.
- The most common bigram in the ciphertext is "QZ" (5 occurrences) which must decipher to either "AE" or "AT". It seems highly implausible that there could be 5 occurrences of "AE" in such a short message, so it must decipher to "AT". That means ciphertext "Z" corresponds to plaintext "T", and ciphertext "T" to plaintext "A".
- Taking advantage of this information and deciphering the whole cryptogram yields:

Figure 26:

- As you can see, we already (with much less work than using frequency analysis alone), have already deciphered much of the cryptogram. We could then continue with a combination of frequency analysis and intelligent guesswork to decipher the rest of the cryptogram.

In short, a crib can gives us a massive head start in breaking a cipher as it essentially provides part of the cipher key "for free" even before we begin frequency analysis. In many cases, we might need to do some frequency analysis before, after, or in combination with the crib, but even in such situations, the crib can significantly assist breaking the cipher.

Defeating Frequency Analysis

For reasonably long messages, frequency analysis is a powerful tool for breaking simple letter and symbol substitution ciphers. However, it is possible to use various techniques to make frequency analysis more difficult or almost impossible

Short Messages

In very short messages, just by chance, certain letters and bigrams can occur much more or less frequently than in typical English text. So, for short messages, frequency analysis may **not** be that helpful in breaking the cipher.

Therefore, one possible strategy for defeating frequency analysis is to confine yourself to sending very short messages. However, this is **not** a very practical strategy in most circumstances:

- It obviously limits how much you can communicate.

- It also does **not** allow you to securely send a series of messages (unless you change the cipher between messages), as an attacker could simply retain copies of every enciphered message and perform frequency analysis on the aggregate text of all the messages.

Homophony

Frequency analysis relies on the fact that in a typical piece of text, some letters are much more common than others. This variation in the frequency of each letter is reflected in both the plaintext and the ciphertext. **Homophony**, which is the idea of having more than one way of enciphering plaintext characters into ciphertext is intended to break this link.

We could for example have a choice of several ciphertext characters corresponding to the plaintext letter "E", and each of the various ciphertext characters would be used at random when enciphering "E". This would mean that "E" would be one of the most common characters in the plaintext, but **not** in the ciphertext. Moreover, we need **not** limit ourselves to using homophony on only one plaintext character – several different (or all) plaintext characters could each have multiple ciphertext equivalents.

Using homophony, at least for the common characters, we can make it much more difficult for an attacker to use frequency analysis to break the cipher. One potential problem is that the ciphertext will need a much larger alphabet of characters than the plaintext, but this can be solved either by creating additional symbols, or by the ciphertext being a sequence of numeric codes and enciphering each plaintext character into one of these codes.

The most powerful use homophony would be to encipher **every** plaintext character in a different way so that no symbol in the ciphertext occurs more than once. This is achievable providing both the sender and the recipient of a cryptogram have access to the **identical** copies of a sufficiently long book (such as the Bible). Each plaintext letter is enciphered into a reference to an appearance of that letter in that book (for example, the page number, line number and word number of a word that begins with the letter). This technique makes frequency analysis completely impossible. The obvious limitation of this idea is that the same book must be accessible to both sender and a recipient but **not** be known **nor** discoverable by an attacker. If an attacker finds out the book that is being used, he can read the messages. These types of ciphers are discussed further in Chapter 11.

Null Characters

Another method of making it harder to use frequency analysis is to use **null characters** ("nulls") Nulls are extra characters that are added to the ciphertext that do **not** correspond to any character in the original plaintext. The purpose of nulls is to confuse the relationship between the frequencies of characters in the plaintext message and the frequencies of characters in the ciphertext.

For example, a very simple scheme using nulls would be to insert an additional random character into every word. Ideally these extra characters would cause the overall frequency distribution of all characters to be as close as possible to even, so that a cryptanalyst would **not** be able to identify common English letters by their higher relative frequency.

Decipherment of epitaph of the Duke Rudolph IV of Austria. The epitaph was written in **Alphabetum Kaldeorum**, which is simple symbolic substitution cipher used in the Middle Ages. Alphabetum Kaldeorum utilises both homophony and null characters:

Other Methods

While frequency analysis is extremely effective against simple substitution ciphers, it is **not** as effective against more sophisticated ciphers. There are many varieties of more sophisticated ciphers which we will look at in the rest of this book, but some ideas that you will encounter in the next few chapters include:

- Rearranging the order of letters so that even if an attacker knows which letters are present, he can **not** reconstruct the letters into a meaningful message (see Chapter 4).
- Spreading information about each plaintext character across multiple ciphertext characters (see Chapter 5).
- Enciphering more than one plaintext character into each ciphertext character (see Chapter 6).
- Using a changing substitution alphabet, such that successive characters within the plaintext are enciphered according to different rules (see Chapter 7).

In the next few chapters, we illustrate each of these techniques with example ciphers. You should also be aware that some ciphers combine multiple techniques for increased security against cryptanalysis.

Chapter 4: Transposition Ciphers

A **transposition cipher** is one in which the ciphertext is generated by rearranging the characters within the plaintext according to some regular system. Transposition ciphers can **not** be broken by using frequency analysis, but the use of one can be spotted by a cryptanalyst because the letter frequencies of the ciphertext will be identical to that of plaintext in the same language.

Scytale

The scytale was a cryptographic device that was used by the Ancient Greeks, especially by the Spartans, during military campaigns. The earliest mention of the device is by Archilocus (c. 680 BC to c. 645 BC) but several other Greek and Roman writers also discuss the scytale.

A scytale was basically just a long wooden rod. A long strip of parchment was wrapped tightly around the rod. Messages would be written horizontally across the wrapped parchment, but when the parchment was unwrapped the letters within the message would be transposed. The parchment would therefore **not** be readable if intercepted while being transported.

To decipher message, the recipient would wrap the parchment around his own rod of equal diameter to the original, and the plaintext message would be revealed.

Rail Fence Ciphers

Rail fence ciphers (also known as **zigzag ciphers**) are very simple transposition ciphers.

To encipher a message using a rail fence cipher, the plaintext is written diagonally downwards and diagonally upwards across the rails of an imaginary fence, and the ciphertext is then obtained by reading off the text in rows. The number of rails used can vary but should always be three or more.

For example, to encipher using a 5-rail rail fence cipher the message "LEAVE AREA IMMEDIATELY PROCEED NORTH AT ONCE":

- Write the message diagonally downwards and upwards across the grid with 5 rows, changing direction each time you hit the bottom or top of the grid:

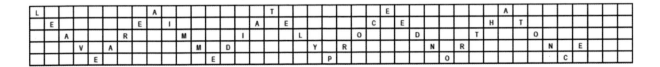

- The ciphertext can then be obtained by reading horizontally row-by-row through the letters. In this case, the ciphertext is "LATEA EEIAE CEHTA RMILO DTOVA MDYRN RNEEE POC" (after arranging the ciphertext letters into groups of five).

To decipher ciphertext (let us say "FPRGU UPSUN LESLE NIOLI NW") that has been enciphered using a rail fence cipher with a known number of rails (let us say 4 in this example):

- Count the total number of characters in the ciphertext (22 in this example).

- Create an empty grid with the same number of columns as the total number of characters (22 in this example) and the same number of rows as the number of rails in the cipher (4 in this example).

- Write the message diagonally downwards and upwards across the grid, changing direction each time you hit the bottom or top of the grid:

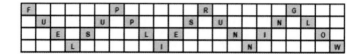

- The plaintext message can be read along the downward and upward diagonals, inserting spaces where necessary. In this case, the plaintext reads "FUEL SUPPLIES RUNNING LOW".

Rail fence ciphers are **not** secure. As there are only a limited range of choices for the number of rails, a cryptanalyst can simply try out each choice until they decipher the message.

Route Ciphers

Route ciphers are a more complex type of transposition cipher.

To encipher a message, the plaintext is written on grid. The ciphertext is then obtained by following a previously agreed route around the grid and reading out the letters in that order.

For example, to encipher "INCREASE ALERT LEVEL AS ENEMY ATTACK IMMINENT":

- Write the plaintext on a grid (for this example, let us assume a grid with 7 columns has been specified, and any left-over cells are to be filled with random letters – shown in green below):

I	N	C	R	E	A	S
E	A	L	E	R	T	L
E	V	E	L	A	S	E
N	E	M	Y	A	T	T
A	C	K	I	M	M	I
N	E	N	T	E	T	A

- The ciphertext is obtained by reading off the characters from the grid along a previously agreed route. For example, let us assume the specified route is "Read the first column vertically from top to bottom, the second column vertically bottom to top, then go to the top right hand corner and go through the remaining characters of the first row right to left, the second row left to right, third row right to left and so on.

Following the specified route through the grid:

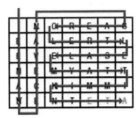

- The ciphertext is obtained by reading out the characters in the order they appear along the route. In this example, the ciphertext is "IEENA NECEV ANSAE RCLER TLESA LEMYA TTIMM IKNTE TA" (after arranging the ciphertext letters into groups of five).

To decipher ciphertext, you begin with an empty grid, and follow the specified route around the grid, filling in ciphertext characters as you go. When you complete the route, the original plaintext message will appear in the grid.

Route ciphers can be very secure against cryptanalysis (provided information about the route used is kept secret) as for reasonably long messages there a vast number of possible routes that could be chosen. However, routes need to be carefully chosen, as a poorly chosen route can lead to words or word fragments being directly visible or simply reversed within the ciphertext.

Columnar Transposition Ciphers

In a **columnar transposition cipher**, the plaintext is written in a grid, the columns of the grid are transposed according to some agreed procedure, and then the ciphertext is obtained by reading out the text column-by-column.

Columnar transposition ciphers often rely on choosing a keyword. Traditionally keywords are chosen with no recurring letters. This keyword serves to specify the number of columns (the same as the number of letters in the word), and how to transpose the columns (the same transposition that would be used to sort the letters of the keyword alphabetically is used on the columns).

For example, let us consider how to encipher "INCREASE ALERT LEVEL AS ENEMY ATTACK IMMINENT" using the keyword "RELIANT":

- Prepare an empty grid with the chosen keyword written above so that one letter of the keyword is above each column:

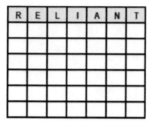

- Write the plaintext message in the grid. The plaintext message may **not** fit exactly, in which case the remaining cells in the grid can either be filled with random characters (a **regular columnar transposition cipher**) or left blank (an **irregular columnar transposition cipher**) as shown in this example:

R	E	L	I	A	N	T
I	N	C	R	E	A	S
E	A	L	E	R	T	L
E	V	E	L	A	S	E
N	E	M	Y	A	T	T
A	C	K	I	M	M	I
N	E	N	T			

- Reorder the columns so that the letters of the keyword are in alphabetic order:

A	E	I	L	N	R	T
E	N	R	C	A	I	S
R	A	E	L	T	E	L
A	V	L	E	S	E	E
A	E	Y	M	T	N	T
M	C	I	K	M	A	I
	E	T	N		N	

- The ciphertext can be obtained by reading through the grid (skipping the keyword letters at the top) column-by-column. In this example, the ciphertext is "ERAAM NAVEC ERELY ITCLE MKNAT STMIE ENANS LETI" (after arranging the ciphertext letters into groups of five).

To decipher ciphertext, you divide the number of characters in the ciphertext by the number of columns to get the number of characters per column. You then fill out the grid column-by-column. Finally, you reorder the columns to their original order so that you can retrieve the plaintext.

Columnar transposition ciphers are potentially vulnerable to attack cryptanalysis. The cryptanalyst begins by guessing the number of columns and on that basis filling out a grid with the ciphertext. He can then look for possible anagrams in any row in order to start to figure out the original column ordering. He may of course need several guesses as to the number of columns in order to break the cipher.

Double Columnar Transposition Ciphers

A **double columnar transposition cipher** is simply a columnar transposition cipher applied twice. The second application can use a different keyword or the same keyword as the first application.

If text has been enciphered in this way, the application of ciphers when deciphering must occur in reverse order to when enciphering:

Double columnar transposition ciphers were used in both World Wars, including by the German Army in World War I, and by the British Special Operations Executive (SOE), the Dutch Resistance, the French Marquis, and the US Office of Strategic Services.

Double columnar transposition ciphers are highly vulnerable to cryptanalysis if multiple messages of the exact same length are sent using the same keywords, as all the messages can be anagrammed simultaneously. This is exactly what the Germans did early in World War I: the French were generally able to break German ciphers of this type and read the messages within a few days. The French however made the mistake of allowing this information to be mentioned in a newspaper, *Le Matin*, and as a result the Germans switched to a different cipher system.

Myszkowski Transposition Ciphers

Myszkowksi transposition ciphers are a variant on columnar transposition ciphers that mix two different kinds of transposition. This cipher was invented in 1902 is named after its inventor, Émile Victor Théodore Myszkowski.

The Myszkowski transposition ciphers relies on choosing a keyword, however the keyword should have one or more recurring letters. This keyword serves to specify the number of columns (the same as the number of letters in the word), and also how to convert the plaintext to ciphertext.

For example, let us consider how to encipher "INCREASE ALERT LEVEL AS ENEMY ATTACK IMMINENT" using the keyword "ATHLETE":

- Prepare an empty grid with the chosen keyword written above so that one letter of the keyword is above each column. Additionally, label each letter of the keyword with its position in alphabetical order within the word (columns containing the same letter will have the same number).

  For example, using the keyword "ATHLETE", the column with "A" will be 1 because "A" is the first letter alphabetically in the keyword, the columns with "E" will both be 2 because "E" is the second letter alphabetically in the keyword, and so on:

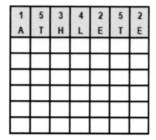

- Write the plaintext message in the grid. The plaintext message may **not** fit exactly, in which case the remaining cells in the grid can either be filled with random characters or may be left blank as shown in this example:

1	5	3	4	2	5	2
A	T	H	L	E	T	E
I	N	C	R	E	A	S
E	A	L	E	R	T	L
E	V	E	L	A	S	E
N	E	M	Y	A	T	T
A	C	K	I	M	M	I
N	E	N	T			

- The ciphertext can be obtained by reading through the grid (skipping the keyword letters at the top). Columns are read through in numerical order:
  - If only one column has a particular number, simply read that column from top to bottom.
  - If two or more columns have the same number, read through each of those columns left to right, and work row-by-row until you have reached the bottom of the grid.

  In this example, the ciphertext is "IEENA NESRL AEATM ICLEM KNREL YITNA ATVSE TCME" (after arranging the ciphertext letters into groups of five).

To decipher ciphertext, you simply start with an empty grid, and instead of reading out cells according to the Myszkowski algorithm, you fill them in. At the end of the process, the plaintext will appear in the grid ready to read out.

Disrupted Transposition Ciphers

Disrupted transposition ciphers are yet another type of transposition cipher. They can produce very complex transpositions that can make cryptanalysis extremely challenging. The key innovation of disrupted transposition ciphers is that the plaintext is **not** inserted into the grid in a straightforward regular fashion.

For example, here is how the plaintext might be entered into the grid in using a disrupted transposition cipher:

- Create an empty grid with your chosen keyword (in this example "ALIMONY") at the top. Ensure the grid is just large enough to accommodate the entire plaintext message (in this example, the plaintext message is 39 letters long, so given we have a 7-letter keyword, we would use a grid with 6 rows, since 7×6 = 42 letters).

A	L	I	M	O	N	Y

- Start writing the plaintext message in the grid row-by-row. However, if at any point, you encounter a letter that is also in the keyword, then start a newline. You will eventually reach the bottom of the grid without completing the plaintext message:

A	L	I	M	O	N	Y
I						
N						
C	R	E	A			
S	E	A				
L						
E	R	T	L			

- Go back to the first row and fill in the remaining cells row-by-row with the rest of the plaintext message. The plaintext message may **not** fit exactly, in which case the remaining cells in the grid can either be filled with random characters or may be left blank as shown in this example:

(cells which were already filled in prior to this step are shown with a grey background)

A	L	I	M	O	N	Y
I	E	V	E	L	A	S
N	E	N	E	M	Y	A
C	R	E	A	T	T	A
S	E	A	C	K	I	M
L	M	I	N	E	N	T
E	R	T	L			

- After filling out the grid in this way, any of the previously mentioned transposition cipher algorithms can be used to generate the ciphertext from the grid. For example, using single columnar transposition algorithm the ciphertext would be "INCSL EVNEA ITEER EMREE ACNLA YTINL MTKES AAMT" (after arranging the ciphertext letters into groups of five).

Grille Ciphers

A **grille** (sometimes known as a **Cardan grille**) is piece of paper, card or a similar object with holes in it, through which the letters or words of a message can be written. Gerolamo Cardano (September 24th, 1501 to September 21st, 1576), who invented these types of grilles, originally proposed by using them as a stenography device (see Chapter 13), but some types of grilles have also been used to generate transposition ciphers.

Trellis Ciphers

Trellis ciphers are a type of transposition cipher where the plaintext is enciphered using a specific type of grille. Sir Francis Walsingham (c. 1532 to April 6th, 1590), the principal secretary to and spymaster for Queen Elizabeth I of England, is known to have used this type of cipher to communicate with some of his agents.

Sir Francis Walsingham:

The grille used for the trellis cipher resembles a chessboard. However, the white squares are perforated so that you can write one plaintext letter through each of these spaces. Traditionally this is done row-by-row. Once all the spaces in the grille have been filled, the grille is rotated or flipped, so that the letters of any remaining plaintext can be added through any unused spaces. Finally, the ciphertext is read column-by-column.

For example, let us consider how to encipher "INCREASE ALERT LEVEL AS ENEMY ATTACK IMMINENT":

- Place the grille and fill-out as much as possible of the plaintext message row-by-row across the white squares:

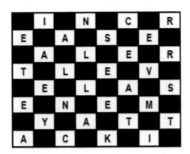

- Flip the grille over while ensuring that the area of the paper covered by the grille remains unchanged. This has the effect of switching black squares for white squares and vice-versa. Then write the remaining part of the message row-by-row across the white squares:

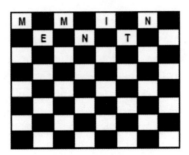

- Fill any remaining white squares with random letters (shown in green in this example):

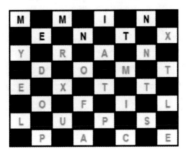

- Remove the grille and you should see a matrix of letters something like this:

```
M  I  M  N  I  C  N  R
E  E  A  N  S  T  E  X
Y  A  R  L  A  E  N  R
T  D  L  O  E  M  V  T
E  E  X  L  T  A  T  S
E  O  N  F  E  I  M  L
L  Y  U  A  P  T  S  T
A  P  C  A  K  C  I  E
```

- The ciphertext can be obtained by reading out the letters column-by-column. In this example, the ciphertext is "MEYTE ELAIE ADEOY PMARL XNUCN NLOLF AAISA ETEPK CTEMA ITCNE NVTMS IRSRT SLTE" (after arranging the ciphertext letters into groups of five).

To decipher a message the process is reversed:
- Write the ciphertext out in a grid column-by-column.
- Place the first grille over the grid and read out the first page of plaintext.
- Place the second grille over the grid and read out the second page of plaintext.

While the trellis cipher does provide very jumbled and transposed ciphertext, it is unfortunately completely insecure. The problem is that once the method is known to an attacker (and it is widely known, including being covered in this book!), it is easy to decipher any cryptogram enciphered in this way.

Fleissner Ciphers

Fleissner ciphers (also known as **turning grille ciphers**) are another method of using a grille to encipher a message. A square Cardano grille with holes cut for single letters is used. The letters of the plaintext message are written through the holes in the grille row-by-row. However, when all the holes have been filled with text, the grille is rotated by 90° (while ensuring that the area of the paper covered by the grille remains unchanged), and the process continues until all four positions have been used (adding random characters at the end if any spaces would otherwise be unused).

Example of using a turning grille cipher:

 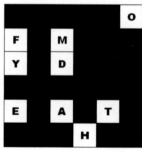 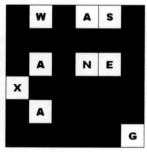 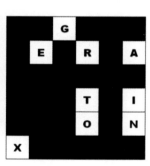

The grille is then removed, and a grid of text is revealed

T	W	G	A	S	O
F	E	M	R	H	A
Y	A	D	N	E	E
X	R	E	T	P	I
E	A	A	O	T	N
X	O	R	H	T	G

The ciphertext is the text on this grid read out column-by-column. In this example, the ciphertext would be "TFYXE XWEAR AOGMD EARAR NTOHS HEPTT OAEIN G" (after arranging the ciphertext letters into groups of five).

It should be noted that any size square grille can be used. However, the positioning of the holes within the grille needs to be carefully thought about: there are some mathematical principles (which we need **not** go into here) to ensuring that each square on the grid is available to write-in once, and once only, while rotating the grille.

Fleissner ciphers are named after Baron Edouard Fleissner von Wostrowitz, an Austrian cavalry officer, who described this type of cipher in his 1881 book, *Handbuch der Kryptographie*. However, Fleissner was **not** the inventor of these types of ciphers, as they are known to have been in use around 150 years earlier and might even have been invented by Gerolamo Cardano in the 16th century. Fleissner ciphers were popularized by the French novelist Jules Verne (February 8th, 1828 to March 24th, 1905), who read Fleissner's book and described the cipher in his own 1885 novel *Mathias Sandorf*.

It has long been known that the security of Fleissner ciphers against cryptanalysis is low. The German Army did briefly use this type of cipher during World War I, but the weakness of the cipher soon became apparent, and the Germans switched to other ciphers after just a few months.

Crossword Ciphers

Another cipher than uses transposition by grille is a crossword cipher. In this type of cipher an empty crossword acts as the grille. Moreover, provided sender and recipient agree which crossword to use (for example, use the cryptic crossword in a particular newspaper on a particular day), it is **not** necessary to keep a conspicuous grille around.

The person sending a message by crossword cipher begins by writing out their message row-by-row in the white squares of an agreed upon crossword:

A	L	P	H	■	A	T	E	A	M	T	O	A	T	T
■	A	■	C	■	K	■	■	A	■	T	■	D	■	A
W	N	B	E	T	A	T	E	A	M	T	O	S	E	C
■	U	■	R	■	E	■	■	F	■	L	■	A	■	N
K	S	G	A	M	M	A	T	E	■	A	M	T	O	P
■	R	■	O	■	V	■	I	■	D	■	E	■	■	C
O	V	E	R	I	N	■	G	F	I	R	E	M	I	S
■	■	S	■	I	■	O	■	N	■	O	■	■	■	■
B	J	E	C	T	I	V	E	■	S	M	U	S	T	B
E	■	■	A	■	C	■	H	■	I	■	E	■	V	■
E	D	R	E	G	■	A	R	D	L	E	S	S	O	F
C	■	O	■	S	■	T	■	A	■	C	■	T	■	■
I	O	N	T	H	I	S	D	A	Y					
	■			■		■			■			■		

Any remaining white squares in the crossword should then be filled out with random letters (shown in this example in green):

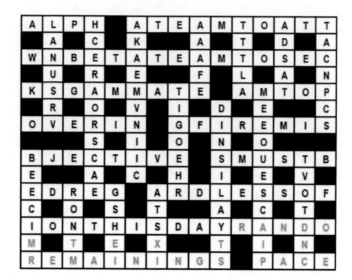

The ciphertext can then be obtained by reading out characters column-by-column. In this example, the ciphertext reads "AWKOB EECIMR LANUS RVJDO EPBGE ERONT MHCER AORSC AETAT MITGS HEIAK AEMVN IICIN TTAVA TSXIE ETIGO EHRDN AAAFE FDAGM MDINS ILAYT STTTL ARMER OOMEE OUESC AIPAD SATMS SNATE OITVO TDNCT ACNPC SBFOE".

Chapter 5: Fractionation and Diffusion

Fractionation is the process of converting each plaintext character into two or more ciphertext characters. For example, each plaintext character can be converted into a two- or three-digit number.

Used alone, fractionation does **not** significantly improve the security of a cipher, since an attacker can simply perform frequency analysis on groups of characters in the ciphertext rather than on individual characters. However, if we rearrange (**transpose**) the order of ciphertext characters according to some pre-agreed rule, this can distribute (**diffuse**) the information about individual plaintext characters over the entire cryptogram. This can make it extremely difficult to perform frequency analysis, as there will be no straightforward relationship between ciphertext characters and plaintext characters.

Bifid Cipher

An example of a cipher that uses fractionation and transposition is the **bifid cipher** which was invented by the French cryptographer Félix Delastelle (January 2nd, 1840 to April 2nd, 1902) in about 1901.

Here is how the bifid cipher is used to encipher a message:

- A Polybius square (see Chapter 1) is created containing the letters of the alphabet.

In this example we use a 5×5 Polybius square, and treat "I" and "J" as if they were the same letter:

	1	2	3	4	5
1	A	Q	U	X	Z
2	F	B	R	V	Y
3	K	G	C	S	W
4	N	L	H	D	T
5	P	O	M	I,J	E

- To encipher a plaintext message such as "SUPPLY DROP AT MIDNIGHT", we begin by finding the coordinates of each letter in the Polybius square:

Each letter is converted into a pair of numbers which are the horizontal (bottom row) and vertical (top row) coordinates of that letter in the Polybius square:

S	U	P	P	L	Y	D	R	O	P	A	T	M	I	D	N	I	G	H	T
3	1	5	5	4	2	4	2	5	5	1	4	5	5	4	4	5	3	4	4
4	3	1	1	2	5	4	3	2	1	1	5	3	4	4	1	4	2	3	5

- We then read out the digits row-by-row. In this case that would be "3 1 5 5 4 2 4 2 5 5 1 4 5 5 4 4 5 3 4 4 4 3 1 1 2 5 4 3 2 1 1 5 3 4 4 1 4 2 3 5".

- We pair up the digits in this list. In this case that would be "31 55 42 42 55 14 55 44 53 44 43 11 25 43 21 15 34 41 42 35".
- The pairs of digits are used as coordinates on the Polybius square to generate the ciphertext.

The encrypted message is generated using pairs of digits as coordinates on the Polybius square:

3	5	4	4	5	1	5	4	5	4	4	1	2	4	2	1	3	4	4	3
1	5	2	2	5	4	5	4	3	4	3	1	5	3	1	5	4	1	2	5
K	E	L	L	E	X	E	D	M	D	H	A	Y	H	F	Z	S	N	L	W

To decipher a message encrypted using the bifid cipher, you simply reverse the process:

- Convert each ciphertext character to a coordinate on the Polybius square.
- Write each coordinate as a vertical pair of numbers.
- When all the coordinates have been written down, read back horizontally the rows of numbers.
- Pair the numbers across each horizontal row.
- Treat each pair as of numbers as a coordinate on the Polybius square, and use that coordinate to find the corresponding plaintext character.

The key element of the bifid cipher is that each character in the plaintext message influences more than one character in the ciphertext. This is illustrated for the first 4 characters of a message in the diagram below.

How each plaintext character effects more than one ciphertext character in the bifid cipher:

| S | U | P | P | L | Y | D | R | O | P | A | T | M | I | D | N | I | G | H | T |

| 3 | 1 | 5 | 5 | 4 | 2 | 4 | 2 | 5 | 5 | 1 | 4 | 5 | 5 | 4 | 4 | 5 | 3 | 4 | 4 |
| 4 | 3 | 1 | 1 | 2 | 5 | 4 | 3 | 2 | 1 | 1 | 5 | 3 | 4 | 4 | 1 | 4 | 2 | 3 | 5 |

| 3 | 5 | 4 | 4 | 5 | 1 | 5 | 4 | 5 | 4 | 4 | 1 | 2 | 4 | 2 | 1 | 3 | 4 | 4 | 3 |
| 1 | 5 | 2 | 2 | 5 | 4 | 5 | 4 | 3 | 4 | 3 | 1 | 5 | 3 | 1 | 5 | 4 | 1 | 2 | 5 |

| K | E | L | L | E | X | E | D | M | D | H | A | Y | H | F | Z | S | N | L | W |

- The "S" at position 1 in the plaintext message is converted to the digits "3" and "4" which in turn contribute to the generation of the 1st and 11th characters ("K" and "H" respectively) in the ciphertext.
- The "U" at position 2 in the plaintext message is converted to the digits "1" and "3" which in turn contribute to the generation of the 1st and 11th characters ("K" and "H" respectively) in the ciphertext.
- The "P" at position 3 in the plaintext message is converted to the digits "5" and "1" which in turn contribute to the generation of the 2nd and 12th characters ("E" and "A" respectively) in the ciphertext.

- The "P" at position 4 in the plaintext message is converted to the digits "5" and "1" which in turn contribute to the generation of the 2nd and 12th characters ("E" and "A" respectively) in the ciphertext.

In the example shown above, you can see each character in the plaintext influences two characters in the ciphertext. This occurs when the message has an even number of characters. When the message has an odd number of characters, each character in the plaintext will influence three characters in the ciphertext, which makes for a more secure cipher.

Finally, you might be wondering how to encipher very long messages using bifid, since it might seem that you would have to convert the entire message into Polybius square coordinates and shuffle this incredibly long list of numbers (which would be time consuming and error prone). For long messages, the normal procedure is the break the message into short fragments of a fixed length (known as **periods**), and then encipher each fragment individually. As is the case for entire messages, fragments which are an odd number of characters in length are more secure than fragments which are an even number of characters in length.

Trifid Cipher

The **trifid cipher** is a cipher that was created by Félix Delastelle in 1902. It improves on his bifid cipher. In trifid, each ciphertext character depends on three plaintext characters plus up to three letters of a keyword phrase.

To begin, we create the cipher key by creating three 3×3 grids:
- Traditionally the three grids are called **layers**, and the cipher key is thought of as a 3×3×3 cube of cells.
- In total, the grids provide 27 cells to accommodate characters. 26 of the cells are filled with the 26 letters of the alphabet and the remaining cell is traditionally filled with a plus sign.
- The standard way to arrange the characters on the grids is by choosing a keyword phrase, filling out the initial cells with that the letters of keyword phrase (skipping any duplicate characters), and then filling the remaining cells with the remaining letters of the alphabet in alphabetic order.

Trifid cipher key created using the keyword phrase "MY SECRET TRIFID KEY":

Layer 1				Layer 2				Layer 3		
	1	**2**	**3**		**1**	**2**	**3**		**1**	**2**	**3**
1	M	Y	S	**1**	D	K	A	**1**	O	P	Q
2	E	C	R	**2**	B	G	H	**2**	U	V	W
3	T	I	F	**3**	J	L	N	**3**	X	Z	+

Each cell on the grid can be referenced by a three-digit number, consisting of its layer number, its row number, and its column number. For example, using grids above:
- 111 would refer to the letter "M".
- 112 would refer to the letter "Y".
- 113 would refer to the letter "S".

- 123 would refer to the letter "R".
- 132 would refer to the letter "I".
- 231 would refer to the letter "J".
- 213 would refer to the letter "A".
- 312 would refer to the letter "P".
- 323 would refer to the letter "W".
- And so on.

To encipher a message using trifid cipher:

- Write out the plaintext message, dividing it into regular length blocks of characters. The block length can be any length, although it is recommended to use a length which is **not** divisible by 3 (Félix Delastelle gave examples with block lengths of 5 and 7 characters in his book).

  For example, the plaintext message "REINFORCEMENTS NEEDED URGENTLY", assuming a block length of 5 would appear:

R	E	I	N	F		O	R	C	E	M		E	N	T	S	N		E	E	D	E	D		U	R	G	E	N		T	L	Y

  Note that the last block may be shorter than the other blocks. You can either just leave that as it is, or you can add some extra random chosen characters on the end to make all blocks the same length.

- Under each letter, write out vertically the three-digit number giving the position of that letter in the cipher key grids:

R	E	I	N	F		O	R	C	E	M		E	N	T	S	N		E	E	D	E	D		U	R	G	E	N		T	L	Y
1	1	1	2	1		3	1	1	1	1		1	2	1	1	2		1	1	2	1	2		3	1	2	1	2		1	2	1
2	2	3	3	3		1	2	2	2	1		2	3	3	1	3		2	2	1	2	1		2	2	2	2	3		3	3	1
3	1	2	3	3		1	3	2	1	1		1	3	1	3	3		1	1	1	1	1		1	3	2	1	3		1	2	2

- Now work through the blocks one-by-one. For each block, you need to group the digits into groups of three, working in horizontal row order, only starting a new horizontal row when you reach the end of an existing row.

  So, in this example, as far as the first block is concerned:
  - The first group of three digits (highlighted below in red) would be 111.
  - The second group of three digits (highlighted below in blue) would 212.
  - The third group of three digits (highlighted below in green) would be 233.
  - The fourth group of three digits (highlighted below in purple) would be 331.
  - The fifth group of three digits (highlighted below in orange) would 233.

R	E	I	N	F		O	R	C	E	M		E	N	T	S	N		E	E	D	E	D		U	R	G	E	N		T	L	Y
1	1	1	2	1		3	1	1	1	1		1	2	1	1	2		1	1	2	1	2		3	1	2	1	2		1	2	1
2	2	3	3	3		1	2	2	2	1		2	3	3	1	3		2	2	1	2	1		2	2	2	2	3		3	3	1
3	1	2	3	3		1	3	2	1	1		1	3	1	3	3		1	1	1	1	1		1	3	2	1	3		1	2	2

The same grouping process also needs to be done for the digits beneath each of the other blocks of letters:

R E I N F	O R C E M	E N T S N	E E D E D	U R G E N	T L Y
1 1 1 2 1	3 1 1 1 1	1 2 1 1 2	1 1 2 1 2	3 1 2 1 2	1 2 1
2 2 3 3 3	1 2 2 2 1	2 3 3 1 3	2 2 1 2 1	2 2 2 2 3	3 3 1
3 1 2 3 3	1 3 2 1 1	1 3 1 3 3	1 1 1 1 1	1 3 2 1 3	1 2 2

- As you group the digits in beneath block, write out each group of digits vertically (I have used colors to indicate which group of three digits creates which vertical column of three digits:

R E I N F	O R C E M	E N T S N	E E D E D	U R G E N	T L Y
1 1 1 2 1	3 1 1 1 1	1 2 1 1 2	1 1 2 1 2	3 1 2 1 2	1 2 1
2 2 3 3 3	1 2 2 2 1	2 3 3 1 3	2 2 1 2 1	2 2 2 2 3	3 3 1
3 1 2 3 3	1 3 2 1 1	1 3 1 3 3	1 1 1 1 1	1 3 2 1 3	1 2 2
1 2 2 3 2	3 1 2 1 2	1 1 3 3 1	1 1 2 1 1	3 1 2 3 2	1 3 1
1 1 3 3 3	1 1 2 1 1	2 2 3 1 3	1 2 1 1 1	1 2 2 1 1	2 3 2
1 2 3 1 3	1 1 2 3 1	1 2 1 3 3	2 2 2 1 1	2 2 2 3 3	1 1 2

- Each vertical three-digit number can be converted back to a letter using the cipher key cube, so this example, the entire ciphertext message would read "MKNXN OMGSD ECXQF YCKMM PCGQA EXC":

R E I N F	O R C E M	E N T S N	E E D E D	U R G E N	T L Y
1 1 1 2 1	3 1 1 1 1	1 2 1 1 2	1 1 2 1 2	3 1 2 1 2	1 2 1
2 2 3 3 3	1 2 2 2 1	2 3 3 1 3	2 2 1 2 1	2 2 2 2 3	3 3 1
3 1 2 3 3	1 3 2 1 1	1 3 1 3 3	1 1 1 1 1	1 3 2 1 3	1 2 2
1 2 2 3 2	3 1 2 1 2	1 1 3 3 1	1 1 2 1 1	3 1 2 3 2	1 3 1
1 1 3 3 3	1 1 2 1 1	2 2 3 1 3	1 2 1 1 1	1 2 2 1 1	2 3 2
1 2 3 1 3	1 1 2 3 1	1 2 1 3 3	2 2 2 1 1	2 2 2 3 3	1 1 2
M K N X N	O M G S D	E C X Q F	Y C K M M	P C G Q A	E X C

To decipher a message encrypted using the trifid cipher, you simply use the exact same process that you used to encipher the message, but instead of the starting from the plaintext, start from the ciphertext:

- Write out the ciphertext in blocks of the agreed length.
- Beneath each ciphertext character vertically write out its coordinates in the cipher cube key.
- Read through the digits under each block in horizontally row-by-row. Group the digits into groups of three and write out each group vertically.
- Treat each vertical three-digit group as a coordinate in the cipher cube key and find the corresponding letter. This is the plaintext letter.

Chapter 6: Polygraphic Substitution

In simple substitution ciphers, each plaintext character is enciphered into one ciphertext character: there is a one-to-one relationship between the characters in the plaintext and the characters in the ciphertext. In **polygraphic ciphers**, the plaintext message is divided into blocks of letters, and each block of letters is enciphered into a single ciphertext character: there is a many to one relationship between the characters in the plaintext and the characters in the ciphertext.

Advantages and Disadvantages of Polygraphic Ciphers

The advantage of a polygraphic cipher is that it can hide the frequency of individual letters, making frequency analysis more difficult. The disadvantage of polygraphic ciphers is that they require a large "alphabet" of ciphertext character symbols.

Let us consider the example of a **bigraphic cipher** (every 2 characters in the plaintext is enciphered into 1 character in the ciphertext) which is used for enciphering just uppercase letters of the English alphabet into cipher text:

- Advantage: There are up to 52 different ways that each plaintext letter can be enciphered. For example, the letter "E" can appear as the first character in a bigram followed by any other character (26 combinations), or it can appear as the second character in a bigram preceded by any other character (a further 26 combinations).
- Disadvantage: we would need 26 × 26 = 676 symbols in the ciphertext alphabet to cover every possible bigram.

The first polygraphic cipher was devised by the Italian polymath Giambattista della Porta (approx. 1535 to February 4th, 1635). della Porta's cipher was based on a very large matrix of symbols. To use the cipher, one would either have had to memorize the entire table (very difficult) or carry around a copy of the table (risky, as an enemy could capture it).

Giambattista della Porta:

Playfair Cipher

The first truly usable polygraphic cipher was created by Sir Charles Wheatstone (February 6th, 1802 to October 19th, 1875) in 1854. Wheatstone's system is known as the **Playfair cipher**.

Sir Charles Wheatstone:

Enciphering and deciphering Playfair messages can easily be performed using pen and paper. It also avoids the need to memorize (or carry around) vast tables of symbols, as it works on pairs of letters (bigrams) treating each pair as if they were one symbol to be enciphered or deciphered.

The cipher is named after Wheatstone's friend Lyon Playfair, first Baron Playfair of St. Andrews, (May 1st, 1818 to May 29th, 1898). Playfair promoted the cipher to the skeptical British Foreign Office, who believed it too complex for use by diplomats. He is said to have offered to demonstrate the system's usability by showing that three out of four boys at a nearby school could learn the system in just 15 minutes. However, the Under Secretary of the Foreign Office responded, "That is very possible, but you could never teach it to attachés."

Lyon Playfair:

The Playfair cipher relies on a 5×5 Polybius square (see Chapter 1). One is created by choosing a keyword and placing it in the initial cells of the Polybius square skipping any duplicate letters in the keyword (So "SECRET" would be entered as "SECRT"). The remaining cells of the Polybius square are filled with all the other letters of the alphabet. As there are 25 cells in the Polybius square and 26 letters in the English alphabet, the letters "I" and "J" are traditionally treated as being the equivalent (some variants treat "K" and "Q" as equivalent)

Polybius square for use with the Playfair cipher preparing using the keyword "SECRET":

S	E	C	R	T
A	B	D	F	G
H	I,J	K	L	M
N	O	P	Q	U
V	W	X	Y	Z

To encipher a message using the Playfair cipher, you begin by dividing your message into two letter bigrams. In the case of a bigram that would otherwise contain a double letter (such as "EE"), insert an extra character (traditionally "X" but "Q" is sometimes used instead) to separate the double letter. You may also need to add an extra character at the end to complete the last bigram. For example, "UNSAFE FLEE NOW" would be arranged into "UN SA FE FL EX EX NO WX" (note the "X"s after the "E"s from "FLEE"" and at the end of the message).

To encipher, you work on each bigram one after another, locating the letters of that bigram within the Polybius square:

- If both letters of a bigram are in the same row of the Polybius square, each plaintext character enciphers into the character one cell to its right (looping around horizontally to the leftmost character if necessary).

  For example, the plaintext bigram "UN" would be enciphered to "NO" (because "N" is to the character we reach by looping around horizontally from "U", and "O" is the character to the right of "N").

S	E	C	R	T
A	B	D	F	G
H	I,J	K	L	M
→N——→O		P	Q	U—
V	W	X	Y	Z

  Similarly, "NO" would be enciphered to "OP" (because "O" is the character to the right of "N", and "P" is the character to right of "O").

S	E	C	R	T
A	B	D	F	G
H	I,J	K	L	M
N——→O——→P			Q	U
V	W	X	Y	Z

- If both letters of a bigram are in the same column, each plaintext character enciphers into the character one cell below it (looping around vertically to the top if necessary).

For example, the plaintext bigram "SA" would be enciphered to "AH" (because "A" is the character below "S", and "H" is the character below "A").

S	E	C	R	T
A	B	D	F	G
H	I,J	K	L	M
N	O	P	Q	U
V	W	X	Y	Z

Similarly, "FL" would be enciphered to "LQ" (because "L" is the character below "F", and "Q" is the character below "L").

S	E	C	R	T
A	B	D	F	G
H	I,J	K	L	M
N	O	P	Q	U
V	W	X	Y	Z

- If the letters are **not** in the same row and **not** in the same column, they define a rectangle of letters by either being the top left and bottom right cells of a such a rectangle, or by being the top right and bottom left cells of the rectangle.

The bigram "FE" defines a rectangle as shown:

S	E	C	R	T
A	B	D	F	G
H	I,J	K	L	M
N	O	P	Q	U
V	W	X	Y	Z

The two plaintext letters in the rectangle are then enciphered to the characters appearing at the horizontally opposite corners:
- If the plaintext letter is at the top left of the rectangle, it is enciphered to the letter at the top right corner.
- If the plaintext letter is at the top right of the rectangle, it is enciphered to the letter at the top left corner.

- If the plaintext letter is at the bottom left of the rectangle, its enciphered to the letter at the bottom right corner.
- If the plaintext letter is at the bottom right of the rectangle, its enciphered to the letter at the bottom right corner.

Hence the bigram "FE" would be enciphered to "BR":

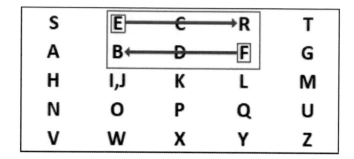

Similarly, the bigram "EX" would be enciphered to "CW":

S	E → C	R	T
A	B D	F	G
H	I,J K	L	M
N	O P	Q	U
V	W ← X	Y	Z

- If we were to perform this process for all the bigrams in "UN SA FE FL EX EX NO WX", the result would be "NO AH BR LQ CW CW OP XY", which after rearranging the letters into groups of five reads "NOAHB RLQCW CWOPX Y",

Deciphering a message in Playfair is simple. You begin by dividing the ciphertext into two-character bigrams, then decipher each bigram one-by-one. To decipher a bigram simply locate the positions of the two ciphertext letters on the Polybius square, and apply the inverse of the operation used to encipher such bigrams:

- If both letters of a ciphertext bigram are in the same row of the Polybius square, each ciphertext character deciphers into the character one cell to its left (looping around horizontally to the rightmost character if necessary).
- If both letters of a cipher text are in the same column, each ciphertext character deciphers into the character one cell above it (looping around vertically to the bottom if necessary).
- If both the ciphertext letters are **not** in the same row and **not** in the same column, they define a rectangle of letters by either being the top left and bottom right cells of a such a rectangle, or by being the top right and bottom left cells of the rectangle. The two ciphertext letters in the rectangle are then deciphered to the characters appearing at the horizontally opposite corners:
- If the ciphertext letter is at the top left of the rectangle, it is deciphered to the letter at the top right corner.

- If the ciphertext letter is at the top right of the rectangle, it is deciphered to the letter at the top left corner.
- If the ciphertext letter is at the bottom left of the rectangle, its deciphered to the letter at the bottom right corner.
- If the ciphertext letter is at the bottom right of the rectangle, its deciphered to the letter at the bottom right corner.

Although better than a simple substitution cipher, the Playfair cipher is **not** secure. It can be broken by a determined human attacker or almost instantly by a computer.

- The first recorded description of how to break a Playfair cipher was published by Joseph Oswald Mauborgne (February 26th, 1881 to June 7th, 1971) of the US Army in 1914.
- Dorothy L. Sayers' 1932 novel *Have His Carcase* contains a detailed description of the Playfair cipher and how to break it.

Joseph Oswald Mauborgne:

Two-Square Cipher

The **two-square cipher** (also known as **double Playfair**) is an improved version of Playfair that relies on two 5×5 Polybius squares placed either side by side (**horizontal two-square**) or one above another (**vertical two-square**). The system was first described in 1901 by Félix Delastelle (who also invented the bifid and trifid ciphers described in Chapter 5).

There are two varieties of the two-square cipher: horizontal and vertical.

To encipher a message using the two-square cipher:

- We first divide our plaintext into bigrams. Unlike the original Playfair, we do **not** need to break double character bigrams by inserting an extra character. We do however still need to add an extra character at the end of the message if the message does **not** have an even number of letters. For example, "UNSAFE FLEE NOW" would be split into ""UN SA FE FL EE NO WX".

- We then encipher each bigram one after another

- If using horizontal two-square, we locate the first character of each bigram in the left Polybius square, and the second character of the current bigram in the right Polybius square.

  If the cells containing the two characters are in the same horizontal row, the ciphertext is simply the two characters in reverse order. For example, the bigram "UN" would be enciphered to "NU".

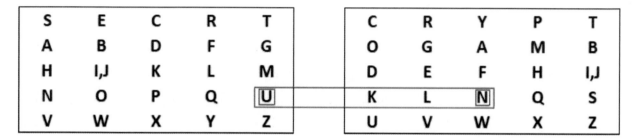

  If the cells containing the two characters are **not** in the same horizontal row, the cells containing the two characters define a rectangle, and each character is enciphered to the horizontally opposite corner of the rectangle. For example, "FL" would be enciphered to GQ":

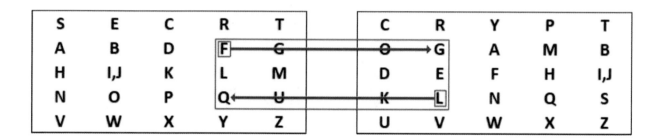

  If we were to perform this process for all the bigrams in in "UN SA FE FL EE NO WX", the result would be "NU YA GL GQ RJ KA XW", which after rearranging the letters into groups of five reads "NUYAG LGQRJ KAXW",

- If using vertical two-square, we locate the first character of the current bigram in the top Polybius square, and the second character of bigram in the bottom Polybius square.

  If the cells containing the two characters are in the same vertical column, the ciphertext is simply the two characters in reverse order. For example, the bigram "NO" would be enciphered to "ON".

S	E	C	R	T
A	B	D	F	G
H	I,J	K	L	M
N	O	P	Q	U
V	W	X	Y	Z

C	R	Y	P	T
O	G	A	M	B
D	E	F	H	I,J
K	L	N	Q	S
U	V	W	X	Z

If the cells containing the two characters are **not** in the same vertical column, the cells containing the two characters define a rectangle, and each character is enciphered to the horizontally opposite corner of the rectangle. For example, "UN" would be enciphered to "PS":

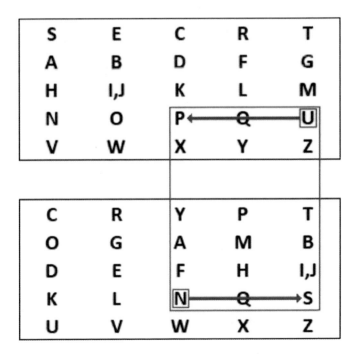

If we were to perform this process for all the bigrams in in "UN SA FE FL EE NO WX", the result would be "PS CO BH BQ EE ON YV", which after rearranging the letters into groups of five reads "PSCOB HBQEE ONYV".

Deciphering ciphertext that has been enciphered using two-square is done by using the same process that is used to encipher the plaintext, but starting from the ciphertext:

- Divide the ciphertext into bigrams.
- Work through the bigrams one-by-one.
- Find the cell containing the first letter of the current bigram in the left (or top) Polybius square and the second letter of the current bigram in the right (or bottom) Polybius square.
- If the cells are in the same row (or column), then the plaintext is simply the bigram in reverse order. For example, if the ciphertext were "EH", it would decipher to plaintext "HE".
- If the cells are **not** in the same row (or column), they will define a rectangle on the Polybius squares, and each ciphertext letter deciphers to the letter in the horizontally opposite corner of the rectangle.

While two-square is marginally more secure than Playfair, it still a relatively weak cipher than can be broken by a computer in seconds and by determined human cryptanalysts, if a sufficiently large corpus of ciphertext is available to review.

During World War Two, the German Army, Air Force and Police used the two-square cipher for medium security messages. The cipher was broken by Allied cryptanalysts working in Bletchley Park, England. Although they would have probably broken the code anyway, Allied efforts were facilitated by German mistakes: The Germans sequentially numbered their messages with the numbers spelled out as words, which provided a powerful set of cribs.

Four-Square Cipher

The **four-square cipher** is another variant of Playfair that uses four 5×5 Polybius squares laid in a 2×2 grid. Traditionally, the top left and bottom right Polybius squares are called plaintext squares and simply contain the alphabet in order, whereas the top right and bottom right have secret arrangements.

A	B	C	D	E
F	G	H	I,J	K
L	M	N	O	P
Q	R	S	T	U
V	W	X	Y	Z

S	E	C	R	T
A	B	D	F	G
H	I,J	K	L	M
N	O	P	Q	U
V	W	X	Y	Z

C	R	Y	P	T
O	G	A	M	B
D	E	F	H	I,J
K	L	N	Q	S
U	V	W	X	Z

A	B	C	D	E
F	G	H	I,J	K
L	M	N	O	P
Q	R	S	T	U
V	W	X	Y	Z

To encipher a message using the four-square cipher:

- We first divide our plaintext into bigrams. Unlike the original Playfair, we do **not** need to break double character bigrams by inserting an extra character. We do however still need to add an extra character at the end of the message if the message does **not** have an even number of letters. For example, "LANDING AT DAWN" would be split into "LA ND IN GA TD AW NX".

- We then encipher each bigram one after another

- Locate the first character of the current bigram in the top right Polybius square, and the second character in the bottom left Polybius square. The cells containing these two characters define a rectangle, and each character is enciphered to the horizontally opposite corner of the rectangle. For example, "LA" would be enciphered to NJ":

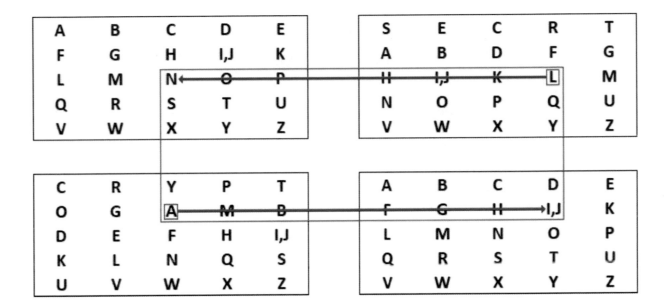

If we were to perform this process for all the bigrams in in "LA ND IN GA TD AW NX", the result would be "NJ QL NR HK AP HV TV", which after rearranging the letters into groups of five reads "NJQLN RHKAP HVTV",

Deciphering ciphertext that has been enciphered using four-square is done by using the same process that is used to encipher the plaintext, but starting from the ciphertext:
- Divide the ciphertext into bigrams.
- Work through the bigrams one-by-one.
- Find the cells containing the first letter of the current bigram in the top left Polybius square, and the second letter of the current bigram in the bottom right Polybius square.
- The cells will define a rectangle on the Polybius squares, and each ciphertext letter deciphers to the letter in the horizontally opposite corner of the rectangle.

Chapter 7: Polyalphabetic Ciphers

A **polyalphabetic cipher** is a cipher based on substitution (see Chapters 2 and 3), but which uses multiple substitution alphabets. As a result, the same plaintext letter may be substituted for a different ciphertext letter in different parts of the same message.

Al-Kindi:

The idea of a polyalphabetic cipher was known to Arab scholars of the Middle Ages. Ibn al-Durayhim (1312 to 1359 or 1362) and Al-Qalqashandi (1355 or 1356 to 1418) both discussed polyalphabetic ciphers in their writings. It has been suggested that that Al-Kindi (801 to 873), who wrote the first description of frequency analysis, may also have been the first person to develop a polyalphabetic cipher.

The first page of Al-Kindi's work "On Deciphering Cryptographic Messages":

Alberti Cipher

The **Alberti cipher** is one of the earliest-known polyalphabetic ciphers. It was devised by Leon Battista Alberti (February 14th, 1404 to April 25th, 1472) and described in his 1466 book *De Cifris*.

Leon Battista Alberti:

To encipher and decipher text, Alberti used a device that he called *Formula*, but which we would nowadays describe as a **cipher disk**. Alberti's cipher disk consisted of two concentric disks both independently moveable about the same central axis. Evenly spaced around the circumference of each disk were numbers and letters. The outer disk contained the plaintext letters in uppercase whereas the inner disk contained the ciphertext in lowercase.

To encipher a message, the following procedure would be used:
- An uppercase letter would be written. This would act as instruction as to how to position the disks relative to each other.
- Each plaintext letter in the message would be located on the outer disk. The adjacent lowercase character on the inner disk would be the ciphertext for that letter.
- Every few characters, the person enciphering was encouraged to reposition the disks and write a new uppercase character indicating the new position, before continuing. In this way, the substitution cipher would be regularly changing throughout the message.
- Alberti also encouraged the use of null characters (see Chapter 3) which could be included in the ciphertext by inserting a digit within plaintext words, minor misspellings to avoid repeated characters, and the replacement of common phrases with a predefined list of numerical codes (since the numerical codes were then enciphered using the disks, these phrases were **superenciphered**, that is enciphered twice).

To decipher a message, you work through the ciphertext character-by-character:
- Whenever you encounter an uppercase letter, you reposition the disks as instructed.
- Otherwise look for the ciphertext character on the inner disk: its plaintext equivalent is the adjacent character on the outer disk.
- Obviously null characters would be skipped over, deliberate misspellings corrected, and numerical codes converted back into words.

Alberti's cipher was immune to frequency analysis and very good at concealing numbers (since they were indistinguishable from letters within the stream of ciphertext), but it was still cryptographically weak. This is because the uppercase letters in the ciphertext signal each change of key (the **key progression**), giving a major clue to cryptanalysts.

Trithemius Cipher

Another early polyalphabetic cipher is the **Trithemius cipher**. It is named for its inventor, Johannes Trithemius (February 1st, 1462 to December 13th, 1516), and was first described in his book *Polygraphiae libri sex*, which was posthumously published in 1518.

Relief on the tomb of Johannes Trithemius:

Polygraphiae was the first printed book on cryptography:

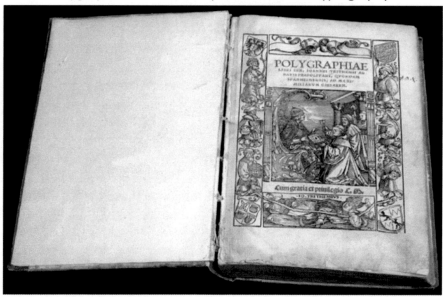

The Trithemius cipher is based around the idea of having many ciphers and switching to a different cipher after each letter of the message. To implement this, Johannes Trithemius relied on a device that he had previously invented in 1508, the **tabula recta**. The tabula recta is a large table drawn on paper, with the letters of the alphabet along the top and left hand side. Each column of the table is filled with the alphabet but shifted by a different amount. The first column is **not** shifted at all, the second column by one letter, the third column by two and so on.

Tabula recta for the modern English alphabet with 26 letters:

(Trithemius used a tabula recta with the Latin alphabet with 24 letters)

	A	B	C	D	E	F	G	H	I	J	K	L	M	N	O	P	Q	R	S	T	U	V	W	X	Y	Z
A	A	B	C	D	E	F	G	H	I	J	K	L	M	N	O	P	Q	R	S	T	U	V	W	X	Y	Z
B	B	C	D	E	F	G	H	I	J	K	L	M	N	O	P	Q	R	S	T	U	V	W	X	Y	Z	A
C	C	D	E	F	G	H	I	J	K	L	M	N	O	P	Q	R	S	T	U	V	W	X	Y	Z	A	B
D	D	E	F	G	H	I	J	K	L	M	N	O	P	Q	R	S	T	U	V	W	X	Y	Z	A	B	C
E	E	F	G	H	I	J	K	L	M	N	O	P	Q	R	S	T	U	V	W	X	Y	Z	A	B	C	D
F	F	G	H	I	J	K	L	M	N	O	P	Q	R	S	T	U	V	W	X	Y	Z	A	B	C	D	E
G	G	H	I	J	K	L	M	N	O	P	Q	R	S	T	U	V	W	X	Y	Z	A	B	C	D	E	F
H	H	I	J	K	L	M	N	O	P	Q	R	S	T	U	V	W	X	Y	Z	A	B	C	D	E	F	G
I	I	J	K	L	M	N	O	P	Q	R	S	T	U	V	W	X	Y	Z	A	B	C	D	E	F	G	H
J	J	K	L	M	N	O	P	Q	R	S	T	U	V	W	X	Y	Z	A	B	C	D	E	F	G	H	I
K	K	L	M	N	O	P	Q	R	S	T	U	V	W	X	Y	Z	A	B	C	D	E	F	G	H	I	J
L	L	M	N	O	P	Q	R	S	T	U	V	W	X	Y	Z	A	B	C	D	E	F	G	H	I	J	K
M	M	N	O	P	Q	R	S	T	U	V	W	X	Y	Z	A	B	C	D	E	F	G	H	I	J	K	L
N	N	O	P	Q	R	S	T	U	V	W	X	Y	Z	A	B	C	D	E	F	G	H	I	J	K	L	M
O	O	P	Q	R	S	T	U	V	W	X	Y	Z	A	B	C	D	E	F	G	H	I	J	K	L	M	N
P	P	Q	R	S	T	U	V	W	X	Y	Z	A	B	C	D	E	F	G	H	I	J	K	L	M	N	O
Q	Q	R	S	T	U	V	W	X	Y	Z	A	B	C	D	E	F	G	H	I	J	K	L	M	N	O	P
R	R	S	T	U	V	W	X	Y	Z	A	B	C	D	E	F	G	H	I	J	K	L	M	N	O	P	Q
S	S	T	U	V	W	X	Y	Z	A	B	C	D	E	F	G	H	I	J	K	L	M	N	O	P	Q	R
T	T	U	V	W	X	Y	Z	A	B	C	D	E	F	G	H	I	J	K	L	M	N	O	P	Q	R	S
U	U	V	W	X	Y	Z	A	B	C	D	E	F	G	H	I	J	K	L	M	N	O	P	Q	R	S	T
V	V	W	X	Y	Z	A	B	C	D	E	F	G	H	I	J	K	L	M	N	O	P	Q	R	S	T	U
W	W	X	Y	Z	A	B	C	D	E	F	G	H	I	J	K	L	M	N	O	P	Q	R	S	T	U	V
X	X	Y	Z	A	B	C	D	E	F	G	H	I	J	K	L	M	N	O	P	Q	R	S	T	U	V	W
Y	Y	Z	A	B	C	D	E	F	G	H	I	J	K	L	M	N	O	P	Q	R	S	T	U	V	W	X
Z	Z	A	B	C	D	E	F	G	H	I	J	K	L	M	N	O	P	Q	R	S	T	U	V	W	X	Y

To encipher a message, the following procedure would be used:

- Look at the first letter of plaintext. Find the row which it heads and read the letter in the first column of that row. (You will find that the letter is unchanged).
- Look at the second letter of plaintext. Find the row which it heads and read the letter in the second column of that row. (You will find that this is equivalent to a Caesar cipher with a shift of one letter).
- Look at the third letter of plaintext. Find the row which it heads and read the letter in the third column of that row. (You will find that this is equivalent to a Caesar cipher with a shift of two letters).
- Look at the fourth letter of plaintext. Find the row which it heads and read the letter in the fourth column of that row. (You will find that this is equivalent to a Caesar cipher with a shift of three letters).
- And so on...

To decipher a message, the reverse procedure would be used:

- Look at the first letter of ciphertext. Find that letter in the first column: the plaintext equivalent is the heading of that row. (You will find that the letter is unchanged).
- Look at the second letter of ciphertext. Find that letter in the second column: the plaintext equivalent is the heading of that row. (You will find that this is equivalent to decipher a Caesar cipher with a shift of one letter).

- Look at the third letter of ciphertext. Find that letter in the third column: the plaintext equivalent is the heading of that row. (You will find that this is equivalent to decipher a Caesar cipher with a shift of two letters).
- Look at the fourth letter of ciphertext. Find that letter in the fourth column: the plaintext equivalent is the heading of that row. (You will find that this is equivalent to decipher a Caesar cipher with a shift of three letters).
- And so on...

The Trimethius cipher is unfortunately a very poor cipher. The problem is that there is no key: once the method of encipherment is known, a cryptanalyst can decipher any message.

Vigenère Ciphers

While the fundamental idea of a polyalphabetic cipher was a good one, the weakness of the Alberti and Trimethius ciphers is that they do **not** conceal the key progression. In the Alberti cipher, the key progression is plainly given away unconcealed within the ciphertext itself, and the in the Trimethius cipher, the key progression is entirely fixed and predictable, and more importantly absolutely identical, in every message ever sent.

Cryptologists do **not** seem to have realized it for some centuries, but the critical element of a secure polyalphabetic cipher was having a secure key progression that could **not** easily be discovered by a hostile cryptanalyst. The most secure keys would be those that repeated infrequently, or better yet, did **not** repeat at all.

The first successful polyalphabetic cipher of this type was the **Vigenère cipher**. The Vigenère cipher is named after the French diplomat Blaise de Vigenère (April 5th, 1523 to February 19th, 1596), who was wrongly attributed with its invention: it was actually invented by Giovan Battisa Bellaso in 1553.

Blaise de Vigenère:

So successful was the Vigenère cipher, that it was long known as *le chiffre indéchiffrable* which is French for "the indecipherable cipher". It took more than three centuries before cryptanalysts found a general way to attack it. Friedrich Kasiski (November 29th, 1805 to May 22nd, 1881) was the first to publish a method in 1863, although Charles Babbage (December 26th, 1701 to October 18th, 1871) probably discovered but did **not** publish the same method in 1854.

Charles Babbage proposed the first digital computer. He is also thought to have figured out how to break the Vigenère cipher in 1854:

To encipher a message using the Vigenère cipher, both sender and receiver must first secretly agree a keyword or keyword phrase. This is used in conjunction with the tabula recta (usually called a **Vigenère square** in this context) to encipher the message.

The tabula recta is called a Vigenère square when used with the Vigenère cipher:

	A	B	C	D	E	F	G	H	I	J	K	L	M	N	O	P	Q	R	S	T	U	V	W	X	Y	Z
A	A	B	C	D	E	F	G	H	I	J	K	L	M	N	O	P	Q	R	S	T	U	V	W	X	Y	Z
B	B	C	D	E	F	G	H	I	J	K	L	M	N	O	P	Q	R	S	T	U	V	W	X	Y	Z	A
C	C	D	E	F	G	H	I	J	K	L	M	N	O	P	Q	R	S	T	U	V	W	X	Y	Z	A	B
D	D	E	F	G	H	I	J	K	L	M	N	O	P	Q	R	S	T	U	V	W	X	Y	Z	A	B	C
E	E	F	G	H	I	J	K	L	M	N	O	P	Q	R	S	T	U	V	W	X	Y	Z	A	B	C	D
F	F	G	H	I	J	K	L	M	N	O	P	Q	R	S	T	U	V	W	X	Y	Z	A	B	C	D	E
G	G	H	I	J	K	L	M	N	O	P	Q	R	S	T	U	V	W	X	Y	Z	A	B	C	D	E	F
H	H	I	J	K	L	M	N	O	P	Q	R	S	T	U	V	W	X	Y	Z	A	B	C	D	E	F	G
I	I	J	K	L	M	N	O	P	Q	R	S	T	U	V	W	X	Y	Z	A	B	C	D	E	F	G	H
J	J	K	L	M	N	O	P	Q	R	S	T	U	V	W	X	Y	Z	A	B	C	D	E	F	G	H	I
K	K	L	M	N	O	P	Q	R	S	T	U	V	W	X	Y	Z	A	B	C	D	E	F	G	H	I	J
L	L	M	N	O	P	Q	R	S	T	U	V	W	X	Y	Z	A	B	C	D	E	F	G	H	I	J	K
M	M	N	O	P	Q	R	S	T	U	V	W	X	Y	Z	A	B	C	D	E	F	G	H	I	J	K	L
N	N	O	P	Q	R	S	T	U	V	W	X	Y	Z	A	B	C	D	E	F	G	H	I	J	K	L	M
O	O	P	Q	R	S	T	U	V	W	X	Y	Z	A	B	C	D	E	F	G	H	I	J	K	L	M	N
P	P	Q	R	S	T	U	V	W	X	Y	Z	A	B	C	D	E	F	G	H	I	J	K	L	M	N	O
Q	Q	R	S	T	U	V	W	X	Y	Z	A	B	C	D	E	F	G	H	I	J	K	L	M	N	O	P
R	R	S	T	U	V	W	X	Y	Z	A	B	C	D	E	F	G	H	I	J	K	L	M	N	O	P	Q
S	S	T	U	V	W	X	Y	Z	A	B	C	D	E	F	G	H	I	J	K	L	M	N	O	P	Q	R
T	T	U	V	W	X	Y	Z	A	B	C	D	E	F	G	H	I	J	K	L	M	N	O	P	Q	R	S
U	U	V	W	X	Y	Z	A	B	C	D	E	F	G	H	I	J	K	L	M	N	O	P	Q	R	S	T
V	V	W	X	Y	Z	A	B	C	D	E	F	G	H	I	J	K	L	M	N	O	P	Q	R	S	T	U
W	W	X	Y	Z	A	B	C	D	E	F	G	H	I	J	K	L	M	N	O	P	Q	R	S	T	U	V
X	X	Y	Z	A	B	C	D	E	F	G	H	I	J	K	L	M	N	O	P	Q	R	S	T	U	V	W
Y	Y	Z	A	B	C	D	E	F	G	H	I	J	K	L	M	N	O	P	Q	R	S	T	U	V	W	X
Z	Z	A	B	C	D	E	F	G	H	I	J	K	L	M	N	O	P	Q	R	S	T	U	V	W	X	Y

For this example, let us assume the chosen keyword is "DIEGO" and the plaintext message to be enciphered is "WE QUELL THE STORM AND RIDE THE THUNDER". You then follow this procedure:

- Write the keyword repeatedly above the plaintext:

- The plaintext is then enciphered letter-by-letter by using the pairs of keyword letters and plaintext letters. For each pair, go to row in the Vigenère square specified by the keyword letter, and to the column specified by the plaintext letter.

For example, to get the first ciphertext character you would look at row "D" column "W" in the Vigenère square and find the ciphertext character is a "Z". Likewise, to get the second ciphertext character you would look at row "I" column "E" in the Vigenère square and find the ciphertext character is a "Z". And so on, until you have processed the entire message.

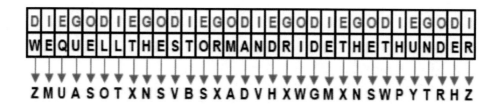

- In this example, the ciphertext is "ZMUAS OTXNS VBSXA DVHXW GMXNS WPYTR HZ" (after arranging the letters into groups of five).

Deciphering text in that has enciphered using the Vigenère cipher is just the same process in reverse:

- Write the keyword repeatedly above the ciphertext.
- The ciphertext is then deciphered letter-by-letter by using the pairs of keyword letters and ciphertext letters. For each pair, go to row in the Vigenère square specified by the keyword letter and find the column containing the ciphertext letter – the plaintext letter is the column heading. Repeat this process for the entire ciphertext.

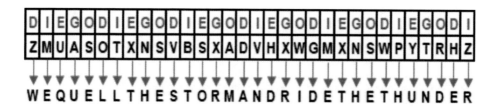

As you can see, the process of encipherment and decipherment is complicated and potentially time-consuming if done entirely manually. However, a cipher disk (or **cipher wheel** containing many disks) can assist with both processes, making the Vigenère cipher suitable for use in field conditions.

Cipher wheel used by the Confederacy during the American Civil War:

As mentioned previously, methods to break Vigenère ciphers were first discovered in the 19th century. The first published method was created by Friedrich Kasiski and is known as **Kasiski examination** (or **Kasiski's test** or **Kasiski's method**). Kasiski examination relies on the fact in a sufficiently long message, some combination of plaintext letters will eventually by chance occur at more than one place under the same keyword letters, and so will therefore be enciphered into in the same ciphertext letters.

For example, if you look at Vigenère ciphertext that we previously considered, you will notice that the plaintext letters "THE" occur under the keyword letters "EGO" at two different places in the same message, and both cases are enciphered into the same ciphertext, "XNS":

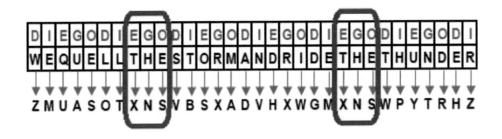

This insight allows a cryptanalyst to determine the keyword length:

- The cryptanalyst looks for repeated sequences of letters in the ciphertext. Any such repeated sequence is almost certainly due to the same plaintext letters being paired with the same part of the keyword.
- The cryptanalyst counts how many letters apart these repeated sequences occur. The keyword length must be a divisor of that distance. In the above example, the first and second occurrences of the "XNS" sequence occur 15 letters apart, which means the keyword length must be 1, 3, 5 or 15 letters.
- In a longer cryptogram, there will be several repeated sequences. Again, the distance in letters between the repeats can be counted, and the keyword length must be a divisor of the distance. For example, if there were a sequence which repeated 20 letters apart, the keyword length would have to be 1, 2, 4, 5, 10 or 20 letters.
- The cryptanalyst simply looks for common divisors of the various repeat lengths. So if repeats occurred at distances of both 15 letters and 20 letters apart, then the keyword length would have to be 1 or 5 letters, since these are the only common divisors of 15 and 20. A keyword length of 1 can be probably be discarded as it would imply the ciphertext was generated using a simple substitution cipher (see Chapter 3), so the keyword length is most likely 5 letters.

Once the keyword length has been established, the ciphertext can be treated as multiple interleaved simple substitution ciphers, each of which can be attacked using frequency analysis. For example, with a keyword length of 5 letters, the cryptanalyst can write out the ciphertext in 5 columns, and then do a separate frequency analysis on each of the 5 columns.

This type of cryptanalysis is highly effective. For example, during the American Civil War, Union cryptanalysts were regularly able to read Confederate messages enciphered using Vigenère ciphers. Using a longer keyword does make cryptanalysis harder, but the only way to completely prevent cryptanalysis is to use a totally random keyword of equal length to the plaintext: this type of cipher is a called a **one-time pad (OTP)**, and is discussed in Chapter 9. Of course, using an extremely long keyword can introduce its own difficulties.

Beaufort and Variant Beaufort Cipher

The **Beaufort cipher** is a cipher created by Rear-Admiral Sir Francis Beaufort (May 27th, 1774 to December 17th, 1857). It is virtually identical to the Vigenère cipher. The only difference is the **Beaufort square** has a different layout from the Vigenère square. In the Vigenère square, the letters in each column are ordered from "A" to "Z", but in the Beaufort cipher the letters are ordered from "Z" to "A".

The most famous use of the Beaufort cipher was in the Hagelin M-209 (known as CSP-1500 to the US Navy and as C-38 by the manufacturer). The Hagelin M-209 was a small and portable mechanical cipher machine used by the United States military in World War II and the Korean War. Over 140,000 of the machines were produced by the Smith Corona Typewriter Company in Groton New York.

The M-209 was just 3¼ inches × 5½ inches × 7 inches (83 mm × 140 mm × 178 mm) and weighed 6 pounds (2.7 kg) for the machine itself, or 7 pounds with the case (3.2 kg). The internals of the machine were entirely mechanical, and could both decipher and encipher messages, printing the output onto paper tape. Using the M-209, experienced operators could encipher or decipher messages at the rate of one letter every 2 to 4 seconds.

M-209 mechanical cipher machine:

The **variant Beaufort cipher** is very similar to the Vigenère cipher and Beaufort cipher. The difference is that whereas one starts with the row/column headings when enciphering using the Vigenère cipher and Beaufort cipher, and the row heading and body of the square when deciphering, in the variant Beaufort cipher, the reverse is done.

Both the Beaufort cipher and the variant Beaufort cipher have the same strengths and weaknesses as the Vigenère cipher, as none of the differences in procedure has any impact on cryptographic security.

Autokey Ciphers

An **autokey cipher** is one which incorporates the plaintext into the key. The key is generated by an algorithm that manipulates the plaintext in some way, such as choosing certain letters from the plaintext, adding a phrase (a **primer**) before the plaintext, or some other automated method.

The earliest known autokey system was developed by Blaise de Vigenère (the same man who is wrongly credited with inventing the Vigenère cipher) in 1586. Vigenère's autokey cipher involved using a single letter as primer and then the plaintext as the rest of the key. In Vigenère's system there were 10 different substitution alphabets, and which should be used at any point depended on successive characters of the key.

One example of simple autokey cipher is that used by the American Cryptogram Association (ACA). The ACA cipher uses a Vigenère square to encipher and decipher the text, with a key that consists of a short primer word, followed the by the rest of the plaintext.

For this example, let us assume the chosen primer is "DIEGO" and the plaintext message to be enciphered is "WE QUELL THE STORM AND RIDE THE THUNDER". You then follow this procedure:

- The key is the primer followed by the plaintext of the message. Write the key above the plaintext (you can leave the last few characters off the end of the key, as you only need to use the part of the key that is that same length as the plaintext).

- The plaintext is then enciphered letter-by-letter by using the pairs of keyword letters and plaintext letters. For each pair, go to row in the Vigenère square specified by the keyword letter, and to the column specified by the plaintext letter.

  For example, to get the first ciphertext character you would look at row "D" column "W" in the Vigenère square, and find the ciphertext character is a "Z". Likewise, to get the second ciphertext character you would look at row "I" column "E" in the Vigenère square, and find the ciphertext character is a "Z". And so on, until you have processed the entire message.

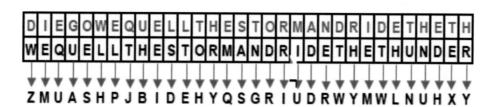

- In this example, the ciphertext is "ZMUAS SOTXN SVBSX ADVHX WGMXN SWPYT RHZ" (after arranging the letters into groups of five).

Deciphering text in that has enciphered using the ACA cipher is essentially the same process in reverse, although you will need to reconstruct the key as you go:
- Write the primer above the ciphertext.

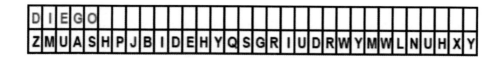

- The ciphertext is then deciphered letter-by-letter by using the pairs of keyword letters and ciphertext letters. For each pair, go to row in the Vigenère square specified by the keyword letter and find the column containing the ciphertext letter – the plaintext letter is the column heading. When you decipher the first letter of the plaintext, you append it to the primer to give the next letter of the key:

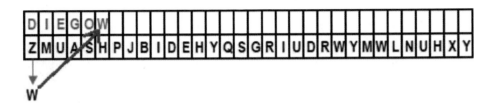

- You then repeat this process for each successive letter of the plaintext. When you decipher the second letter of the plaintext, you also append it to the known part of the key (as shown below) and so on until the entire cryptogram is deciphered.

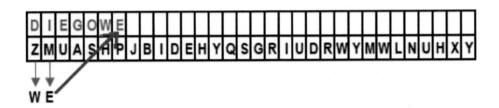

In general, autokey ciphers are more secure against cryptanalysis than polyalphabetic ciphers with fixed keys (such as the Vigenère and Beaufort ciphers), because the key does **not** repeat within a message. However, because the key contains plaintext, the cipher is vulnerable:

- The cryptanalyst chooses common words and letter combinations that are highly likely to occur as part of the plaintext. For example, if the plaintext is known to be in English, the attack might begin by trying "THE", and later perhaps try words such as "AND" or "YOU".
- The cryptanalyst tries their word or letter combination at every possible location in the key, seeing what the corresponding part of the ciphertext would decipher to, in that case. The cryptanalyst is looking for locations that would produce something which might plausibly be part of the plaintext.
- Through a process of trial and error, that involves working out all the consequences of the key containing the guessed word or letter combination, the cryptanalyst can gradually reconstruct more and more of the plaintext and of the key.

Chapter 8: Enigma

The story of Enigma is one of the most famous and celebrated stories in cryptanalysis. It is also a case where cryptanalysis had a huge impact on the course of historical events.

The Enigma Machine

Enigma was a machine for enciphering and deciphering messages invented by German engineer Arthur Scherbius (October 30th, 1878 to May 13th, 1929) just after World War I. Scherbius patented the idea for a cipher machine in 1918 and began marketing the machines under the brand *Enigma* in 1923. The machines were initially offered to commercial users, but they were later adopted by various government and military users, including the German military from 1926 onwards. Over the next two decades various improvements and changes were made in successive models of the machine but the fundamental principles of operation remained unchanged.

Drawing from Scherbius' 1928 US patent:

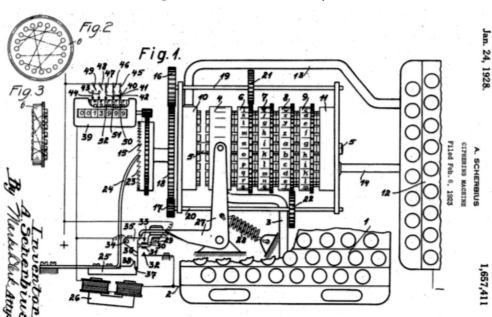

The general principle of Enigma was that messages would be enciphered by the sender using the machine and then transmitted by Morse code over the radio as encoded ciphertext. The recipient would transcribe the Morse code, and then enter it into their own Enigma machine to decipher the message. The radio signals could of course be intercepted by the German's enemies, but the Germans (wrongly) believed that their messages were secure, since they did **not** think that Allied cryptanalysts would be able to break the cipher.

The Enigma machine outwardly resembled a typewriter. Above the keyboard was a **lampboard** with the twenty-six letters of the alphabet.

- To encipher a message, an operator would type the plaintext on the keyboard. Each key pressed on the keyboard would cause one of the letters on the lampboard to light up. A second operator would transcribe the letters on the lampboard as they were lit up and thus record the ciphertext. Some machines could be fitted with an optional accessory, the *Schreibmax*, which printed the ciphertext on a narrow strip of paper, thus eliminating the need for a second operator.
- To decipher a message, the exact reverse procedure would be followed: an operator would type the ciphertext on the keyboard, and the plaintext would be displayed on the lampboard or printed to the *Schreibmax*. A patented feature (called the **reflector**) in all but the very earliest Enigma machines ensured that the machines were self-reciprocal and there was no separate encipherment and decipherment modes. If you enciphered plaintext on one machine and then entered the ciphertext on a second identically configured machine, you would get the original text back. A consequence of this design was that no letter could ever be enciphered as itself, which eventually (as we shall see) turned out to be a crucial cryptographic weakness in the machine which Allied cryptanalysts exploited.

The internal operation of Enigma was electromechanical, which means that it involved both electrical and mechanical components. Pressing a key on the keyboard completed an electrical circuit which caused one of the lights on the lampboard to illuminate. The innovation of Enigma was that the circuit varied (and thus which key caused which light to illuminate) depending on both the initial configuration of the machine and as the message was typed. Or to put it another way, Enigma implemented a polyalphabetic substitution cipher, and the substitutions used constantly changed in a way that seemed impossible for an attacker to know or predict.

M4 Enigma machine:

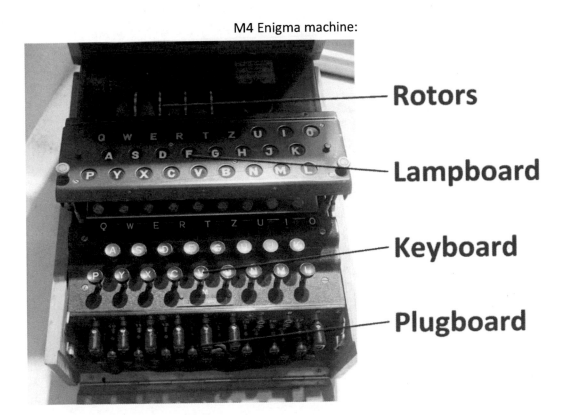

Some of the ways in which the circuit could vary included:

- There were several rotors within the machine. Each rotor had 26 different positions that it could be placed in, and each key press would cause one or more of the rotors to rotate to a new position. At each position of each rotor, the electrical pathway between each key and the lampboard would be different. Moreover, Enigma machines generally had more rotors available than slots for rotors (for example, three rotors from a selection of eight could be inserted into an M4 Enigma machine), and the selection, order, and initial positions of the rotors, could all be varied. Complicating things still further, the position of the alphabet relative to each rotor could also be varied.
- Most military machines also had a **plugboard**. The plugboard allowed wires to be inserted that connected various pairs of sockets at the front of the machine in numerous possible combinations, and these wires added even more possible variations to the circuit.
- Some machines also had additional settings that could be varied. For example, in some machines, the wiring of the reflector (the component which ensured the machine was self-reciprocal) could be varied, and in the M4 Enigma machine, the reflector was split into a thin reflector and an additional rotor which could be positioned in any of 26 positions.

Enigma rotors:

As you can see, there are a vast number of ways that the circuit could be set up. The three-rotor Enigma that was used by the German Army (Heer) and Germany Airforce (Luftwaffe) had for example 158,962,555,217,826,360,000 possible configurations. This meant that even if an attacker had an intercepted message and fed it into their own Enigma machine, unless they also knew the exact configuration used when enciphering, they would **<u>not</u>** be able to decipher the message. The vast number of configurations meant that a **brute-force attack** (trying every possible configuration)

on the cipher was impractical, and so the Germans were confident that the Allies would **not** be able to read their enciphered messages.

The Germans distributed key lists telling their operators how to configure their Enigma machines each day. These key lists were protected as highly secret (for example were **not** allowed to be transported on aircraft) since if captured would compromise all messages sent with that type of machine. Hence the notice "Attention! Key material must not fall into enemy hands intact. In case of danger destroy thoroughly and early.":

Geheime Kommandosache! Jede einzelne Tagesschlüssel ist geheim. Mitnahme im Flugzeug verboten! Nr. 00190

Luftwaffen-Maschinen-Schlüssel Nr. 649

Achtung! Schlüsselmittel dürfen nicht unversehrt in Feindeshand fallen. Bei Gefahr restlos und frühzeitig vernichten.

Tag	Walzenlage			Ringstellung			Steckerverbindungen an der Umkehrwalze	Steckerverbindungen am Steckerbrett										Kenngruppen			
								1 2 3 4 5 6 7 8 9 10													
31	I	V	III	14	09	24		SZ GT DV KU FO MY EW JN IX LQ										wny dgy	exb rzg
30	IV	III	II	05	26	02		IS EV MX RW DT UZ JQ AO CH NY										ktl acw	zsi wzo
29	III	II	I	12	24	03	KM AX PZ OO	DJ AT CV IO ER QS LW FZ FN BH										ioc zcn	ovw wvd
28	II	III	V	06	08	16	DI CN BR PV	GR FV AI DK OT MQ EU BX LP GJ										woj fbh	vct uis
27	III	I	IV	11	03	07	LT EQ HS UW	DY IN BV GR AM LO PP HT EX UW										xle gbo	uev rxm
26	I	IV	V	17	22	19		VZ AL RT KO CG EI BJ DU FS HP										ouc uhq	uew uit
25	IV	III	I	08	25	12		OR FV AD IT PK HJ LZ NS EQ CW										kpl rwl	vci tlq
24	V	I	IV	05	18	14		TY AS OW KV JM DR HX GL CZ NU										ebn rwm	udf tlo
23	IV	II	I	24	12	04		QV FR AK EO DH CJ MZ SX GN LT										jqc acx	mwe wve
22	II	IV	V	01	09	21	IU AS DV GL	PJ ES IM RX LV AY OU BO WZ CN										jpw del	mwf wvf
21	I	V	II	13	05	19	PT OX EZ CH	RU HL FY OS OZ DM AW CE TV NX										jqd cef	nvo ysh
20	III	IV	V	24	01	10	MR KN BQ PW	OX PR FH WY DL CM AE TZ JS GI										idf fpx	jwg tlg
19	V	III	I	17	25	20		EJ OY IV AQ KW FX MT PS LU BD										lsa zbw	vcj rxn
18	IV	II	V	15	23	26		IR KZ LS EM OV OY QX AF JP BU										mae hri	sog ysi
17	I	IV	II	21	10	06		HM JO DI NR BY XZ OS PU FQ CT										tdp dhb	fkb uiv
16	V	II	III	08	16	13		DS NY MR GW LX AJ BQ CO IP NT										ldw hzj	soh wvg
15	II	IV	I	01	03	07		GM JR KS IY HZ PL AX BT CQ NV										imz noa	tjv xtk
14	IV	I	V	15	11	05	AI BT MV HU	LY AG KM BR IQ JU HV SW ET CX										zgr dgz	gjo ryg
13	I	III	II	13	20	03	PW EL DQ KN	MU BP CY RZ KX AN JT DG IL PW										zdy rkf	tjw xtl
12	V	II	IV	18	10	07	RZ OQ CP SX	KN UY HR PW PM BO EZ QT DX JV										zea rjy	soi wvh
11	II	IV	III	02	26	15		LR IK MS QU HW PT OO VX FZ EN										lrc zbx	vbm rxo
10	III	V	IV	23	21	01		QY BS LN KT AP IU DW HO RV JZ										edj eyr	vby tlh
9	V	I	III	16	04	08		PI NQ SY CU BZ AH EL TX DO KP										yiz dha	ekc tli
8	IV	II	V	13	19	25		UX IZ HN BK GQ CF FT JY MW AR										lan dgb	zsj wbi
7	I	IV	II	09	03	22		DQ GU BW NP HK AZ CI PO JX VY										lao cft	zsk wbj
6	III	I	V	11	18	14	IL AF EU HO	MV CL GK OQ BI FU HS PX NW EY										lju cdr	iye waj
5	V	II	IV	23	02	25	QT WZ KV GM	AC BL OZ EK QW GP SU DH JM TX										lsb zby	vcy ujb
4	II	IV	I	04	21	09	BF NR DX CS	KR MF CN BF EH DZ IW AV GJ LO										lap owd	iwu wak
3	V	I	II	19	11	06		BN HU EG PY KQ CP OS JW AI VZ										aqd bdy	iyf xtd
2	IV	V	I	16	14	02		DP BM NZ CK OV HQ AF UY SW JO										kgl cdf	giq wuv
	II	I	III	23	12	10														

How Enigma was Broken

Despite the German's confidence in their system, thousands of messages sent using Enigma (and other German cipher systems) were deciphered by Allied cryptanalysts in a secret program known as Ultra. The Ultra program gave Allied leaders access to many of Germany's most secret communications and plans, and thus provided a significant advantage in the conduct of the war. Some of the key successes attributed to Ultra include:

- Allowing Allied ships and aircraft to attack Axis supply convoys in the Mediterranean. Lack of supplies blunted Rommel's offensive across Egypt, so Ultra was possibly decisive in stopping the Germans from reaching Cairo and the Suez Canal.
- Allowing Allied convoys in the Battle of the Atlantic to avoid German submarine wolfpacks, and conversely guiding Allied antisubmarine forces towards German U-boats. While other Allied technical advances and the sheer scale of American naval construction would probably have ultimately ensured Allied victory anyway, without Ultra losses of ships and men would have been far higher.

- Enabling the Allied deception plan that tricked Germans into thinking a second larger invasion would come after D-Day. As a result of this, the Allies did **not** have to face the strongest German forces in the West in the first crucial days and weeks after D-Day.

The Ultra program was based at Bletchley Park in Buckinghamshire, England:

While these and other contributions by Ultra were important, the overall scale of the advantage that Ultra provided is still a subject of debate among historians. What can be said with certainty is that Allied leaders considered Ultra to have been crucial to victory. Western Allied Supreme Commander Dwight D. Eisenhower (October 14th, 1890 to March 28th, 1969) considered it "decisive", and British Prime Minister Winston Churchill (November 30th, 1874 to January 24th,1965) said "It was thanks to Ultra that the we won war."

General Dwight D. Eisenhower addressing paratroopers prior to D-Day:

The story of Allied efforts against Engima shows that even apparently unbreakable ciphers can be broken. Moreover, it also illustrates the dangers of complacency in cryptography. Among the reasons why the Allies were able to break Enigma were several key weaknesses in the machine's design, as well as many sloppy German procedures and habits that provided important clues for Allied cryptanalysts.

Early British Efforts

Enigma machines became available to purchase commercially in the 1920s. One such machine was purchased in 1925 in Vienna by Alfred Dillwyn "Dilly Knox" (July 23rd, 1884 to February 27th, 1943), who had previously been involved in breaking the cipher of the Zimmerman telegram (see Chapter 14) during World War I.

The machine as evaluated by Hugh Rose Foss (May 13th, 1902 to December 23rd, 1971) of the Government Code and Cipher School (GC&CS). Foss wrote a paper entitled "The Reciprocal Enigma" discussing how to solve the non-plugboard version of Enigma. Overall, Foss concluded the machine had "a high degree of security" but the cipher could be attacked if short sections of plaintext could be guessed.

Knox later worked on deciphering Enigma messages. At first, he only had messages that he had generated himself to work on, but by the late 1930s he could study radio intercepts of messages sent by Germany's allies. During the Spanish Civil War (1936 to 1939), Germany supplied Enigma machines to the Spanish Nationalists and the Italian Navy. Although the German military, starting with the German navy (Kriegsmarine), had adopted a version of Enigma with a plugboard in 1926, the machines supplied to the Spanish and Italians lacked a plugboard.

Knox was first able to solve one of the Spanish messages on April 24th, 1937. He used a technique that he called **buttoning up** to figure out the wiring of the rotors in the machine. To decipher the messages, he used a second technique which he called **rodding**. Rodding was based on many of the ideas first described by Foss, relying heavily on cribs and crossword solving.

Once Knox was able to read the Spanish and Italian messages, he began to work on messages sent from Spain to Germany using machines with a plugboard. This however was a much more difficult task.

The Polish Cipher Bureau

In 1928, Polish monitoring stations began intercepting machine-enciphered messages broadcast on German radio stations. Cryptanalysts were instructed to try to decipher these messages but were unable to do so. At around the same time, the Polish Cipher Bureau (Biuro Szyfrów) realized that mathematicians might make good cryptanalysts and began to teach a cryptology course to mathematics students at Poznań University. Three of these mathematics students, Marian Rejewski (August 16th, 1905 to February 13th, 1980), Henryk Zygalski (July 15th, 1908 to August 30th, 1978) and Jerzy Różycki (July 24th, 1909 to January 9th, 1942) would eventually make key contributions to breaking Enigma.

The Polish Cipher Bureau was initially based in the General Staff Building (Saxon Palace) in Warsaw:

Marian Rejewski made the first breakthrough in 1932. At that time, when sending a message, the sending German operator would configure the machine according to a **daily key**, and then choose a three-letter code as the **message key** (also known as an **indicator**) so that all messages of the day were **not** enciphered in the same way. The message key was sent using the daily key, before the main message, the machine would be reconfigured using the message key in combination with the daily key, and then the actual content of the message was then sent. The recipient would do the reverse: he would set up his machine initially with the daily key, he would decipher the message key using the daily key, and then reconfigure his Enigma machine with the combination of message key and daily key before deciphering the rest of the message.

Marian Rejewski:

The Germans however made a crucial mistake in their procedures which Rejewski was able to exploit. Concerned that that there might be errors in the transmission of the three-letter message key, it was sent twice in a row before the main message. This introduced a major cryptographic weakness, as the first and fourth ciphertext letters, the second and fifth ciphertext letters, and the third and sixth ciphertext letters were encipherments of the same plaintext letter using the daily key. This was all the information that Rejewski needed to make a breakthrough.

Rejewski studied the first six letters of the ciphertext messages intercepted each day. For example, if one message began "BGYTHQ", then Rejewski knew that "B" was related to "T", "G" to "H" and "Y" to "Q". Another message would give him another set of relationships between letters, for example that "T" was related to "E". Yet another message might tell him that "E" was related to another letter and so on. This method, which he called the **method of characteristics**, allowed Rejewski to put together cycles of 3, 4, 5, 6, or more related letters, and from these cycles deduce much about the cipher. In part, this was possible because Rejewski knew that no letter could be enciphered as itself. Of course, each day a new daily key would be applied, the configuration of the Enigma machines would be updated, and a new set of cycles would apply.

Using the letter pairs in the six-letter prefix at the start of Enigma messages (examples shown), Rejewski was able to construct cycles of related ciphertext letters:

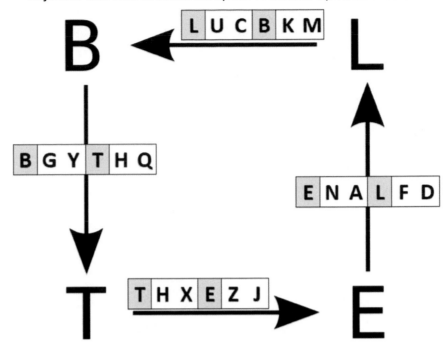

An additional tool that Rejewski was able to use was the German operators did **not** tend to choose their message keys at random, but often used predictable combinations (known to the Allied cryptographers as **cillies** but pronounced "sillies"). For example, operators often used the initials of a girlfriend, the same letter three times in a row (example: "AAA"), or three horizontally or diagonally adjacent keys on the keyboard. Using such information and by applying his skill in pure mathematics, Rejewski was able to reduce the description of the wiring Enigma to a system six equations, albeit with many unknown variables.

At this point, Rejewski was uncertain whether his system of equations would be solvable. Years later, after the war, Rejewski reminisced that although he did have a method to proceed, it was "imperfect and tedious" and relied on chance. An analysis in 2005 by mathematician John Lawrence suggested that if he had continued upon this path, it probably have taken Rejewski four years or more to deduce Enigma's wiring.

However, other sources of information soon became available. Rejewski was able to use information gleaned from the commercial version of Enigma , some inspired guesswork, and key help from French military intelligence, to deduce the wiring of the machine and eventually break the cipher.

- Although it was somewhat different to the version of Enigma used by the German military, Rejewski had access to a commercial version of the machine to study. In the commercial Enigma, the connections were wired in German keyboard order ("QWERTZ..."), but in the military machine the connections were wired differently. Rejewski, perhaps noting the German penchant for order, correctly guessed that the connections in the military machine would be wired in alphabetic order ("ABCDE...").
- A spy within the German cryptographic service, Hans-Thilo Schmidt (May 13th, 1888 to September 19th, 1943), codenamed Asché or Source D, supplied section of D of French

military intelligence with documents about Enigma. This information was then in turn passed on by the French intelligence officer Gustave Bertrand (December 17th, 1896 to May 23rd, 1976) to the Polish Cipher Bureau and Rejewski. Among the information were the daily key settings for September and October 1932, and crucially, these key settings spanned a period during which the rotors were changed.

Gustave Bertrand (pictured here after World War II) of Section D of French military intelligence (the Deuxième Bureau de l'État-major général) provided crucial information about Enigma:

By the beginning of 1933, despite **not** having access to a military Enigma and without having a single machine or rotor to examine, Rejewski had deduced the wiring of the machine – the information was so good, that the Cipher Bureau was able to instruct a Polish manufacturer to produce duplicate machines (**Enigma doubles**) based on these specifications. However, Rejewski was still **not** able to decipher Enigma messages without having the daily keys supplied by one of Gustave Bertrand's spies. Rejewski, Zygalski and Różycki knew that they could **not** rely on a spy supplying that information so now addressed that problem. Rejewski later commented that previously he had had the keys and had to solve the machine, but now the situation had reversed: he had the machine but had to solve the keys.

The Poles were able to determine the majority of the machine's settings (which were determined by the key) by examining the initial six characters of each cryptogram, the doubled message key. However, some settings still remained to be determined in order to obtain the complete daily key and thence to decipher the German messages. Fortunately, another German mistake provided the opening that the cryptologists need. Most German messages began "ANX" (German for "To" followed by an "X" to indicate a space), so the Poles simply tried every possible three-letter combination (there are 17,576 such combinations) to see which corresponded. This was known as the **grill method**. Once this was found, the Poles could read every message sent by the Germans that day.

In 1934 or 1935, Rejewski came up with the idea of creating a catalog indexed by the cycle lengths determined by the method of characteristics. The catalog was printed on index cards and contained 105,456 permutations (the Poles ignored a few complicated cases). The idea was that the cryptanalyst could look up those cards (usually one or just a few) with the correct cycle lengths, and the card would give the rotor order and position. Creating the card catalog was long and laborious procedure that took over a year even with the help of a specially designed machine (called a **cyclometer**). However, once the catalog was created, the Poles could obtain the daily keys with only about 15 minutes work.

Drawing of Rejewski's cyclometer:

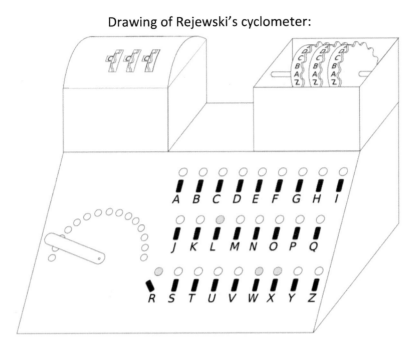

At the beginning, the task of breaking the code was relatively easy. The Germans always paired up twelve letters using six plugboard leads (**steckers**). Moreover, they limited themselves to just three rotors and only changed the order quarterly. However, over time the Germans gradually improved their procedures making changes that the made it harder and harder to break the daily keys.

- In February 1936, the Germans started changing the order of the rotors monthly instead of quarterly.
- In October 1936, the Germans started changing the order of the rotors daily instead of monthly. Additionally, they changed the number of plugboard leads from six to a variable number between five and eight. This change made the grill method less effective, but the card catalog method was **not** impacted.
- In May 1937, the German navy, which was more security conscious than other parts of the German military, introduced a new procedure for the message keys that was more secure than that used previously. As a result, messages sent by the German navy were **not** readable by Allied cryptanalysts for several years. However, the German Army and German Airforce continued to use the existing message key procedure, so their messages remained vulnerable.
- In November 1937, the Germans introduced a new reflector with different wiring. This invalidated the entire card catalog. The Poles immediately set about recalculating the entire catalog and creating a new set of index cards. This was done quickly, and by January 1938, they were once again reading about 75% of intercepted Enigma messages. Moreover, Rejewski is on the record as saying that with a small increase in personnel, they could have read 90% of intercepted Enigma messages.
- On September 15th, 1938, the Germans made changes to the procedures used on all Enigma networks except for the network operated by the Nazi security agency, the Sicherheitsdienst

(SD), who waited until July 1st, 1939 before changing. As a result of this change, the method of characteristics stopped working. Fortunately, the Germans did continue with the insecure practice of sending the message keys twice, and the Poles were able to exploit this. Henryk Zygalski came up with a manual method that involving overlaying specially prepared perforated sheets (**Zygalski sheets**) with the holes corresponding to possible positions of the rotors. As more and more sheets were overlaid, the number of apertures that went through all the sheets gradually reduced, and eventually there would be only a single aperture remaining, whose position was indicative of the cipher key. Meanwhile Rejewski designed a machine called the **bomba kryptologiczna** (plural: **bomby**) or **cryptologic bomb** based on Enigma that could solve the keys. Six such bomby were required, corresponding to the six possible rotor orders. The bomby were built and ready for use by mid-November, and with them, the Poles could solve the keys and begin reading the day's messages within about two hours.

- On December 15th, 1938, the Germans increased the total number of rotors from three to five (with three of the five rotors being placed in the machine). In order to have a chance at continuing to decipher German messages, the Poles needed to figure out the wiring of the two new rotors. Luckily, since the SD had **not** updated their procedures yet, Rejewski was able to do this by examining their messages. However, there was a bigger problem remaining: whereas Enigma had previously only had six possible rotor orders, there were now sixty. Each possible rotor order required a different bomba but building sixty bomby was far beyond the Poles' resources (it would cost fifteen times the Cipher Bureau's entire annual budget). Similarly, they also now needed sixty sets of Zygalski sheets, but that too was beyond the capabilities of the small Polish team.

- On January 1st, 1939, the Germans increased the number of plugboard leads to seven to ten (from the previous five to eight). The bomby depended on unconnected letters on the plugboard, so this further decreased their usefulness. However, the Zygalski sheet method was independent of the number of plugboard connections, so was **not** impacted.

Zygalski sheet:

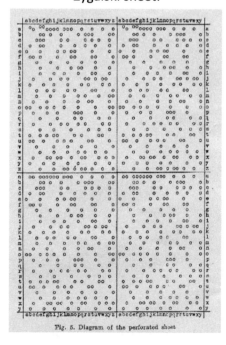

Fig. 5. Diagram of the perforated sheet

Polish Cooperation with the Western Allies

In 1938, as war clouds gathered over Europe, the British Government Code and Cipher School (GC&CS) began to discuss Enigma with French military intelligence. The French provided the British with the details of the military Enigma that had been supplied their spy, Asché, signal intercepts made in Eastern Europe, and information about their links with the Polish Cipher Bureau.

A Polish-French-British meeting was arranged in January 1939 to take place in Paris. Attending from the British side were Dilly Knox, Hugh Foss and Commander Alexander "Alastair" Guthre Denniston (December 1st, 1881 to January 1st, 1961). The Polish team were under orders **not** to disclose their discoveries about Enigma, leaving the British disappointed. However, Dilly Knox did describe his rodding method. This impressed the Poles and they requested his presence at the next meeting.

A German-Polish Non-Aggression Pact had been signed in 1934. It required the two states to settle disputes peacefully by negotiation for the next ten years and provided for Germany to effectively recognize Poland's borders. In October 1938, the German foreign minister, Joachim von Ribbentrop (April 30th, 1893 to October 16th, 1946) proposed a renewal of the pact, in exchange for Germany being allowed to annex the Baltic port city of Danzig and gaining an extraterritorial road and railroad through Polish territory. On April 28th, 1939, after Poland had refused, German leader Adolf Hitler unilaterally abrogated the Non-Aggression Pact.

The Germans demanded to annex Danzig (outlined in purple), and to have an extra territorial road and railroad link between western Germany (outlined in pink on the left) and the German exclave of East Prussia (outlined in pink on the right) through Polish territory (outlined in green):

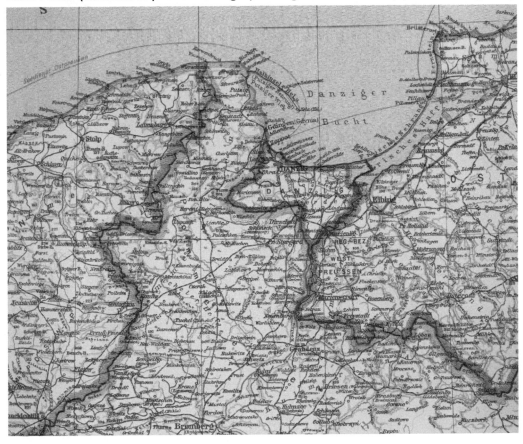

By the Summer of 1939, with war **not** only looking likely but imminent, the Poles decided to share what they had learned about Enigma with their allies. A second meeting with the British and French cipher breakers was held in the Kabaty Woods near Warsaw on July 25th and July 26th, 1939. At this meeting, the Poles revealed that they had broken Enigma and how they had done it. Moreover, the Poles promised to give each of both Britain and France a Polish-made Enigma double, as well details of all their equipment including Zygalski sheets and the bomby. In return, the British, who had more resources than the Poles, promised to prepare complete sets of Zygalski sheets covering all sixty rotor wheel orders.

One fact that was revealed at the meeting surprised the British. As you will recall, the commercial version of Enigma had connections wired in the "QWERTZ" order of German typewriters. The British had been stymied in their attacks on the German Enigma by **not** knowing its wiring. Dilly Knox was shocked when Rejewski revealed that it was simply alphabetic "ABCDE" order, a possibility that he himself had rejected as being too obvious!

Of more serious concern was the fact that the Polish system relied on the message key being sent twice. Dilly Knox was worried that the Germans might switch to a different system of sending message keys and therefore the Allies' ability to read Enigma messages might "at any moment be cancelled".

PC Bruno

On September 1st, 1939, Germany invaded Poland. This was the start of World War II in Europe, as after Germany ignored an Anglo-French ultimatum to withdraw, Britain and France declared war on Germany on September 3rd, 1939.

Within days of the start of the invasion, it became apparent that Poland would be unable to stop the German invasion. On September 5th, 1939, the Cipher Bureau started to destroy files and equipment, and began to evacuate personnel. On September 19th, the Cipher Bureau personnel crossed Poland's southeastern border into neutral Romania. From there, they were able to cross in Yugoslavia, then Italy, before eventually arriving in France.

By October 1939, the Poles had set up a joint program (PC Bruno) with the French. PC Bruno was initially was based at Château de Vignolles in Gretz-Armainvilliers, which is about 25 miles (40 km) southeast of Paris. The effort was commanded by Gustave Bertrand who had now been promoted to Major. Staffing included 50 Frenchmen, 7 anti-fascist Spaniards, and 15 Poles including Marian Rejewski, Henryk Zygalski and Jerzy Różycki.

The British wanted the Polish cryptologists to come to Bletchley Park where own Britain's program was located. However, the Polish commander, Lieutenant Colonel Langer, took the view that the since the Polish Army in exile was forming in France (many of the troops having escaped via the same Romanian route used by the cryptologists), the Cipher Bureau should be located in the same country.

Even though the Poles did **not** come to Bletchley Park, they did cooperate closely with the British. A special telegram line was set up between Bletchley Park and PC Bruno. To ensure security of the communications between the two locations, Enigma itself (using the Polish Enigma doubles) was used to encipher such messages. Messages from PC Bruno to Bletchley were typically padded with innocuous words and ended with an ironic "Heil Hitler!"

In January 1940, British cryptologist Alan Turing (June 23rd, 1912 to June 7th, 1954) visited PC Bruno and brought with him a complete set of Zygalski sheets that had been prepared by one of his colleagues at Bletchley Park, John Jeffreys (January 25th, 1916 to January 13th, 1944). As a result of this, on January 17th, 1940, the Poles successfully deciphered a wartime Enigma message for this first time. Initially, the cryptologists were only able to read old Enigma messages (from October 28th, 1939), but by March both PC Bruno and Bletchley were able to break some German keys and read some Enigma messages at the same time as the intended German recipients. These deciphered messages gave the Allies advance notice of the German invasions of Denmark, Norway, the Netherlands, Belgium and France, but the Allies were unable to make effective use of this information.

Statue of Alan Turing at the University of Surrey:

On May 10th, 1940, the Germans launched their long-awaited offensive in the West against the Netherlands, Belgium and France. Immediately before the offensive, the disaster that Dilly Knox had predicted happened: the Germans stopped transmitting the Enigma message keys twice. This meant that the Zygalski sheet method no longer worked. The Allies were however able to still able to decipher some Enigma messages because of poorly chosen messages keys. Such poor chosen messages keys included ones that were predictable combinations (cillies) and ones where the operator used the rotor position at the end of the previous message as the key for the next message. The Allies called the latter the **Herival tip**, after John Herival (August 29th, 1918 to January 18th, 2011), who had first guessed that some lazy Enigma operators might do this.

The 1940 campaign in the West did **<u>not</u>** go well for the Allies, with the Germans breaking through Allied lines with a surprise attack through the Ardennes region. In the early hours of the morning on June 10th, 1940, as the Germans approached, Gustave Bertrand evacuated PC Bruno. On June 22nd, France surrendered to the Germans. On June 24th, Bertrand used three planes to fly the Polish and anti-fascist Spanish staff to French Algeria.

Cadix

The armistice with the Germany divided France into an occupied zone, and an unoccupied "Free Zone". Bertrand secretly returned to France in September 1940 and set up a new cipher bureau codenamed Cadix at Uzès on the Mediterranean Sea coast in the "Free Zone". The staff of Cadix included 9 Frenchman, 15 Poles and 7 Spaniards.

Cadix also had a branch office in Algeria, which periodically exchanged staff with Uzès. Several Cadix staff, including Jerzy Różycki, were unfortunately lost in one of these exchanges when the passenger ship *Lamoricière* sank on January 9th, 1942.

The new bureau continued the work of breaking German ciphers until November 1942. On November 8th, 1942, the Allies landed in French North Africa ("Operation Torch"), and when the French authorities there did **<u>not</u>** seriously resist, the Germans responded by occupying the "Free Zone" in southern France. On realizing what was about to happen, Major Bertrand evacuated Cadix on November 9th, and many of the staff attempted to escape to Allied territory. Rejewski and Zygalski escaped to Spain, and after being imprisoned for a while, eventually made it to Britain. Some other members of the Cadix staff were **<u>not</u>** so fortunate, and five of the Poles were captured by the Germans. However, all the cryptologists who were captured kept the secret so the Germans did **<u>not</u>** discover that the Allied had deciphered Enigma.

The Allies landed in French North Africa in November 1942:

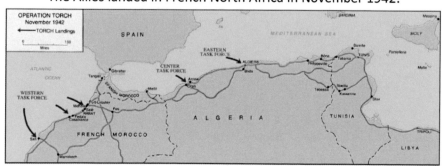

British Efforts Against Italian Naval Enigma

During the Spanish Civil War, British cryptologists had broken the Italian Navy's version of Enigma, which lacked a plugboard. When Italy entered the war, Dilly Knox wanted to know if the Italians were still using the same system. He therefore instructed his assistants to use his rodding technique and the crib of "PERX" (Italian for "for" followed by an "X" to indicate a space) to see if they were.

For three months nothing was found using this technique but then Mavis Lever (May 5th, 1921 to November 12th, 2013) found that the first four letters of a message deciphered using rodding were "PERS". Despite orders to proceed no further, she kept going and found the plaintext "PERSONALE" (Italian for "personal"). Lever's discovery confirmed that the Italians' procedures and cipher equipment were unchanged.

In March 1941, Lever deciphered an Italian message containing the text "today's the day minus three". Working day and night, Lever and her colleagues then discovered that Italians were planning to attack a British convoy moving from Cairo in Egypt to Greece, and even obtained the detailed Italian plan of attack. As a result of this intelligence, ships of the British Royal Navy and the Royal Australian Navy intercepted the Italian fleet and were able to win a decisive victory at the Battle of Cape Matapan between March 27th and March 29th, 1941. Moreover, the British took care **not** to reveal that they had broken Italian ciphers, by using one of their reconnaissance planes to "spot" the Italian fleet.

British Fairey Swordfish torpedo bombers attack the Italian cruiser Bolzano during the Battle of Cape Matapan:

Workers at Bletchley Park were rarely congratulated for their performance or told about the successes that resulted from their intelligence, but this occasion was an exception. A few weeks after the Battle, Admiral Cunningham (January 7th, 1883 to June 12th, 1963) who had commanded the Allied fleet, visited Bletchley Park to congratulate Dilly Knox and his team.

The British Focus on Cribs

Just as the Polish Cipher Bureau had, the British Government Code and Cipher School realized the value of mathematicians as cryptologists. Among the mathematicians recruited was Alan Turing, who was a Fellow of King's College Cambridge. Turing began working part-time for GC&CS around the time of Munich Crisis in September 1938, and reported for duty at Bletchley Park on September 4th, 1939, the day after Britain declared war on Germany.

As already mentioned, Turing visited PC Bruno in January 1940. Like Dilly Knox, Turing was worried that the Polish method for breaking Enigma relied on the Germans repeating each message key twice, something which they could (and eventually did) stop doing. Therefore, Turing initially focused on finding alternative ways to decipher Enigma that did **not** rely on the German's continuing to make this mistake.

The British eventually developed cryptological processes that were based around cribs. For example, a crib could be tried against every possible position in the ciphertext (a process that the British called **crib-dragging**) with the knowledge that Enigma never allowed a letter to be enciphered as itself.

Finding cribs became a major part of the effort at Bletchley Park and a special Crib Room was set up for this purpose. Some of the methods that the British used to find cribs included:

- They kept detailed records of previous messages so they could be analyzed for possible future cribs. The information was indexed in multiple ways, including by message preamble, the names of people, names of ships, military units, weapons, technical terms and so forth. Also recorded was the date and time of the intercept, its radio frequency, the call sign of the radio stations and so forth.
- Looking for common and stereotypical phrases used in German messages such as "an die gruppe" ("to the group"), "keine besonderen ereignisse" ("nothing to report"), and weather station numbers (such as "weather survey 0600"). Additionally, some individuals had a habit of writing their messages in a standard way – for example, the Quarter Master serving Field Marshal Erwin Rommel (November 15th, 1891 to October 14th, 1944) always prefixed his messages with the same formal introductory text.
- Looking for messages which were retransmissions of previous messages. Sometimes the Germans used Enigma to rebroadcast a message that they had previously been sent using a less secure cipher (one that the Allies could read) or that they had sent on another Enigma network (again a network which the Allies could read). The cryptologists at Bletchley Park called this a **kiss**, because they recorded the relevant messages with an "X".
- Nathalie "Lily" Sergueiew was a German spy in Britain who had been turned and worked for the British MI5 intelligence service. While in British employ, she did help deceive the Germans about the location of the D-Day landings, but perhaps of more significance is the help she gave in breaking Enigma. Long messages were sent in her name (either by her herself or by MI5 on her behalf), which the Germans then re-enciphered and transmitted using Enigma. Since the British knew the exact content of these messages, they served as an excellent crib.

- The British would sometimes plant a crib in a practice known as **gardening**. For example, the Royal Air Force would drop sea mines in a specific location, and the Allied cryptologists would then await a message announcing the German discovery of the mines with the grid reference, and a subsequent "all clear" message.
- Captured German Enigma operators were interviewed. By this method it was discovered that the operators had been instructed to spell numbers out rather than using the previous practice of using the top row of the keyboard ("Q" for "1", "W" for "2" and so on). Alan Turing then reviewed previously deciphered messages and discovered that they almost always contained "eins" (German for "one").

British Bombe and American Bombes

Like the Poles, and most likely inspired by them, the British quickly turned to automation to accelerate their cipher breaking efforts. In September 1939, Alan Turing designed an electromechanical device he called a **bombe** to assist in crib-based deciphering of Enigma messages. The bombe was designed to uncover the daily settings of German Enigma machines including the rotors in use and their positions, the starting positions of the rotors, the message key, and the wirings of the plugboard.

The engineering and construction work of the bombe was done by Harold Hall "Doc" Keen (1894 to 1973) of the British Tabulating Machine Company (BTM) who turned Turing's ideas into a practical machine. The first bombe, which was named *Victory*, was installed in Bletchley Park on March 1st, 1940. A second machine with improvements to the design (these same improvements were later retrofitted to *Victory*), which was named *Agnus Dei*, *Agnes* or *Aggie* entered service on August 8th, 1940. Eventually over 200 British bombes (albeit varying in features) would be built by BTM.

A British bombe in Bletchley Park:

The British and United States began cooperating even before the US entered the war in December 1941. Whereas the British cryptanalytic effort was a combined services operation, the United States had two different cryptanalytic services: the Signals Intelligence Service (SIS) of the US Army and OP-20-G of the US Navy. Representatives of both services (Captain Abe Sinkov and Lieutenant Leo Rosen of the US Army, and Lieutenants Robert Weeks and Prescott Currier of the US Navy) made an extended visit to Bletchley Park beginning in February 1941. The Americans gave the British a replica of the Japanese cipher machine known as "Purple", and in return the British gave them a radio direction finding unit (RDF) and numerous documents including a description of Enigma.

Analog of a "Purple" cipher machine constructed by the US Army Signals Intelligence Service:

Despite some initial caution by senior British figures who were concerned that the Axis might discover that their ciphers were being broken, a good working relationship was established between cryptanalysts of both nations. Eventually the British shared the secret of the bombe with their new ally. Colonel John Tiltman (May 25th, 1894 to August 10th, 1982), who later became the Deputy Director of Bletchley Park, visited the US in April 1942, including a visit to the OP-20-G office. Likewise, US Naval Lieutenants Joseph Eachus and Robert Ely visited Bletchley Park in July 1942 and were given complete blueprints and wiring diagrams of the bombe.

British cryptologists John Tiltman (right), with Harry Hinsley (left) and Edward Travis (center) in Washington DC in November 1945.

Funding for a US Navy program of bombes was approved on September 4th, 1942. The contract for construction of US Naval bombes was awarded to the National Cash Register Corporation (NCR). Alan Turing visited the United States in December 1942, including visits to OP-20-G and NCR, and was able to offer advice on the US program. The first US machine as completed and tested on May 3rd, 1943. A total of 121 bombes were constructed for the US Navy before production was stopped in September 1944, and they played an important role in breaking German naval codes.

US Navy bombe:

The US Army also developed their own version of a bombe. The US Army bombe was created by Bell Telephone Laboratories and was known as *003* or *Madame X*. US Army bombes were considerably different from the British or US Navy bombes and specialized in very rapidly solving 3-rotor Enigma ciphers.

While they differed in detail, all the bombes relied on cribs. They would deduce Enigma settings and keys based on the combination of plaintext in known to be in a message and established Enigma characteristics (for example that a letter could **not** be enciphered as itself, and that two letters connected on the plugboard could only be exchanged with each other and **not** with a third letter). Once the Enigma settings were deduced it would then be possible to read all messages sent on that Enigma network for the day (or two days in the case of the German Navy) could be read.

Choosing a crib and setting up a bombe was highly skilled process. This was because the bombe searched for Enigma settings that deciphered the ciphertext to yield the crib and then stopped, but multiple stops would be found in a typical search. Although all the stops would reveal the crib, most were **false stops** that would **not** decipher the rest of the message. There would be one **true stop** that would decipher the entire message and finding it would require testing out each of stops one-by-one until the true stop was reached. Making efficient using of the bombes required minimizing the number of false stops and optimizing the search process.

Alan Turing performed a complicated probability analysis linking the crib length, the rotor order, and the plugboard letter pairing, which assisted cryptanalysts in making best use of the bombes. Even with this information, a cryptanalyst would still need devise a search procedure (known as a **menu**) and configure the bombe to use the menu by arranging patch cables on the rear of the machine.

A graphical illustration of a bombe menu. Each green circle represents the relationship between a suspected plaintext letter (from the crib) and a ciphertext letter. Each blue rectangle indicates the position of that letter in the cryptogram. In this example, the cryptanalyst suspects ciphertext "W" at position 1 corresponds to plaintext "A", ciphertext "S" at position 2 corresponds to plaintext "T", and so on. This example contains three closed loops (known as **closures**). The more closures in a menu, the less false stops would occur.

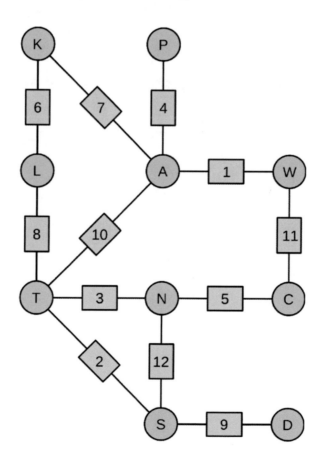

Another issue that the cryptanalysts faced was completing the search within a reasonable time. Several optimizations were developed to facilitate this, including:

- As we have described previously, there were many possible orders for the rotor wheels. However, to decrease time needed by the bombe, cryptanalysts could omit some of these wheel orders from the search. Some of the Enigma networks had rules about **not** repeating a recently used rotor order, or **not** putting the same rotor in the same slot on two consecutive days: while intended to enhance security, these measures actually reduced it, by decreasing the number of rotor combinations that Allied cryptanalysts needed to check. For German Navy messages, a process called **Banburismus** had been devised by Alan Turing and was used to identify the most likely right and middle wheels. Banburismus relied on a mistake in the design of Enigma: each turning rotor had notches that determined when to trigger the turning of the next rotor (called **turnover**), but because the notches were placed differently on each rotor, it was possible to guess the presence of a particular rotor by when turnover did **not** occur.

- Gordon Welchman (June 15th, 1906 to October 8th, 1985), who like Turing was a Cambridge University mathematician, realized that since the plugboard always reciprocally swapped pairs of letters (if "X" was swapped to "Y", then "Y" would be swapped to "X"), bombes could be modified to use this fact to drastically reduce the number of Enigma settings that needed to be searched. The device that implemented this discovery was called the **diagonal board** and it was incorporated into all British bombes.

- The German Airforce had a rule that did **not** allow two adjacent letters to be connected on the plugboard. While this rule was intended to increase security, it actually reduced it, as once the British became aware of the rule, the number of possible plugboard combinations that needed to be searched was greatly decreased. A special feature called the **consecutive stecker knockout** was incorporated into 40 of the British bombes to take advantage of this German mistake.

No original British bombes are believed to survive, but a replica was reconstructed between 1995 and 2006, and is today on display at The National Museum of Computing in Bletchley Park:

German Suspicions

The Allies were always careful to arrange things such that there was another plausible explanation for any intelligence or military advantage that they received as a result of breaking Enigma. Some German leaders, most notably Großadmiral Karl Dönitz (September 16th, 1891 to December 24th, 1980), did have suspicions at times. However, the Germans generally remained confident in the security of Enigma until the very end of World War II, even though the Allies were at that point deciphering and reading almost all Enigma traffic within a day or two.

Karl Dönitz in charge of U-boats from 1935 to 1943, and overall Commander in Chief of the German Navy from 1943 to 1945:

One example of the cat and mouse game is the events of Operation *Rheinübung* ("Exercise Rhine"), a planned raid on British merchant ships by the German Navy. On May 18th, 1941, the German heavy cruiser *Prinz Eugen* sailed from Gotenhafen (today Gydnia in Poland), followed a day later by the battleship *Bismark*. On May 21st, 1941, the two warships briefly stopped at Grimstadfjord (which is near Bergen) in Norway, before proceeding towards the Atlantic shipping lanes on May 22nd. The Germans assigned five tankers, two supply ship and two scout ships to support the warships. After sinking the *Bismark*, the British Royal Navy directed its forces to attack the support ships, but deliberately decided **not** to target the tanker *Gedania* and the scout *Gonzenheim*, so that the Germans would **not** realize that they were reading Enigma. However, quite by chance, British ships did encounter the *Gedania* and *Gonzenheim*, and sank them both. As a result of these events the Germans did investigate whether Enigma had been breached but concluded it had **not**. Nevertheless, they did take measures to improve the security of Enigma by for example disguising grid locations within Enigma messages and giving the U-boats their own separate Enigma network.

Another close shave for the British was the capture of the German U-boat *U-570* in August 1941. Although the German Navy knew of the vessel's capture, they assumed that the crew would have destroyed all the important documents. This was **not** the case – documents captured including signals in ciphertext and their plaintext equivalents, and the U-boat commander's handbook which explained the meanings of the abbreviations and jargon used in the signals.

In early 1942, the German Navy improved the security of Enigma, and as a result the U-boats became more successful in attacking Allied shipping. This could have given the Germans a clue that the Allies had previously been reading their messages, but they attributed their increased success to other factors – principally that the United States had entered the war, and that the U-boats were able to attack many easy targets near the US East coast.

Capture of U-570 by the Royal Navy (photograph from a Royal Air Force Catalina aircraft):

Again in 1943, there should have been hints that the Allies were reading Enigma. Indeed, Karl Dönitz himself suspected as much. The Allies were having increased success in hunting U-boats, and German cryptanalysis of Allied communication signals showed that the Allies were able to estimate the sizes of wolfpacks of U-boats with surprising accuracy. German investigators however concluded that the Allies had **not** broken Enigma but had developed improved direction-finding equipment. Nevertheless, the Germans remain suspicious and further improved the U-boat Enigma.

The Germans attributed increased Allied success in tracking U-boats to the development of improved direction-finding equipment such as the cavity magnetron, an example of which was retrieved by the Germans from a downed Allied bomber in 1944:

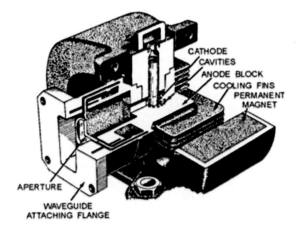

Chapter 9: Perfect Ciphers

Cryptanalysts attack substitution ciphers by trying to figure out the substitutions used. In the case of Caesar ciphers (see Chapter 2) and simple substitution ciphers (see Chapter 3),the substitutions can be found relatively easily by analyzing the ciphertext. Attacks on polyalphabetic ciphers such as the Vigenère and Beaufort ciphers (see Chapter 7), autokey ciphers (see Chapter 7), and Enigma (see Chapter 8) were also based on figuring out the substitution alphabets. These attacks rely on the fact that the sequence of substitution alphabets repeats (Vigenère and Beaufort ciphers), or is partly guessable (autokey ciphers), or comes from physical machine whose workings can be determined through mathematical analysis (Enigma).

This suggests an idea for a perfect (**information-theoretically secure**) polyalphabetic cipher: use a sequence of substitution alphabets (one per letter in the plaintext) that have no pattern but are completely random chosen. When used properly, such a cipher can **not** be broken even if an adversary has unlimited computing power. Claude E. Shannon (April 30th, 1916 to February 24th, 2001), known as the "father of information theory", described this as **perfect secrecy** because the ciphertext reveals nothing about the plaintext.

The sequence of substitution alphabets is the key for this type of cipher. Although the cipher itself is secure against cryptanalysis, the practical weakness of this approach is that the key is very long (it must contain at least as many characters as the entire message) and can only be used once. The problem then becomes how to securely make these very long keys available to both transmitter and recipient without interception by a third party.

Vernam Cipher

In 1919, Gilbert Sanford Vernam (April 3rd, 1890 to February 7th, 1960) an engineer at AT&T Bell Labs patented a teleprinter cipher system for use with Baudot code (see Chapter 1). Vernam's patent, US Patent 1,310,719, has subsequently been described by the US National Security Agency (NSA) as "one of the most important in the history of cryptography". The ideas in the patent form the basis of the perfect ciphers described in this chapter, and hence sometimes these types of ciphers are called **Vernam ciphers** (although the term Vernam cipher is also sometimes used to refer to any type of cipher than works on a stream of data).

As you will recall, each character in Baudot code consists of five bits each of which may be positive or negative. Vernam's idea was to combine each bit of the plaintext with one bit of a key. The key would thus need to have the same number of bits as the plaintext, or if measured in characters (each character being five bits), the same number of characters. As a combining function, Vernam proposed using the **exclusive or (XOR)** Boolean operation (you can read more about Boolean operations in my book Advanced Binary for Programming & Computer Science).

The XOR operation combines two bits of input (in this case one bit from the plaintext and one bit from the key) to produce a single output bit.

- If one or the other input bit is positive, but **not** both, then the output is positive.
- If both input bits are positive, then the output is negative.
- If both input bits are negative, them the output is negative.

This is shown below:

Inputs		Output
Plaintext	Key	Ciphertext
-	-	-
-	+	+
+	-	+
+	+	-

Similarly, a group five bits corresponding to a plaintext character in Baudot code can be XORed one-by-one with another group five bits corresponding to a key character in Baudot code to produce five bits corresponding to a ciphertext character also in Baudot code. An example of this is shown below:

Plaintext	C	+	-	+	+	-
Key	H	+	+	-	+	-
Ciphertext	I	-	+	+	-	-

The beauty of the XOR operation for this purpose is it reversible by simply reapplying the same process to the ciphertext as to the plaintext (**symmetric**):

- To convert plaintext to ciphertext: XOR the plaintext with the key.
- To convert ciphertext to plaintext: XOR the ciphertext with the key.

Since the key is potentially very long, Vernam suggested that it be provided on punched paper tape (of the type suggested by Donald Murray – see Chapter 1) to both the transmitter and recipient of the message.

Diagram from the 1919 Vernam's 1919 patent:

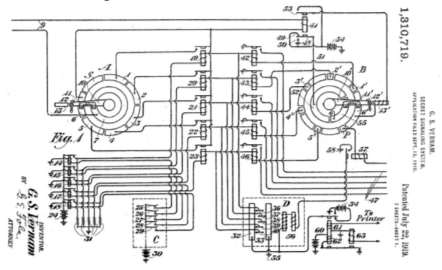

While Vernam proposed the basis for a cryptographic device providing perfect secrecy, the description in his patent did **not** quite achieve it. The patent proposed using identical tape loops with the key at both ends. The weakness of this idea being that the key repeats and therefore the ciphertext can be attacked using the same method as the Vigenère cipher.

Joseph Oswald Mauborgne, who we previously encountered in Chapter 6 as being the first person to break the Playfair cipher, came up with the critical improvement. Instead of a looped tape, Mauborgne suggesting using a paper tape at least as long as the message, that never repeated and containing completely random data. With these enhancements, it is impossible for an attacker to determine the key by examining the ciphertext, so the cipher provides perfect secrecy.

Noreen (also known as BID 590) was a cipher machine with a one-time random tape key. It was used by the British and Canadians from the mid-1960s until 1990:

One-Time Pads

A **one-time pad (OTP)** is another device for providing perfect secrecy. The idea again is that each successive letter of a message is enciphered using a different substitution alphabet, and there is no pattern to the substitution alphabets used. The key is the pattern of substitution alphabets, and perfect secrecy occurs providing the choice of substitution alphabets is truly random and never repeats. The idea of a one-time pad was first created in 1882 by Frank Miller (1842 to 1925).

One-time pads can be implemented using pen and paper (or sometimes typewriter and paper) with pre-prepared pads providing the substitution alphabets to use, or they can be implemented by physical device such as a teleprinter or computer terminal. The Vernam cipher machine, provided Mauborgne's enhancement is used, is in terms of information theory, identical to a one-time pad cipher implemented with pen and paper. As a result, these types of ciphers that can provide perfect secrecy are known as **Vernam ciphers** (although some sources use the term Vernam cipher to refer to a wider range of ciphers that work on a stream of data) or as **one-time pads**.

An example of a one-time pad that can be used to encipher or decipher messages using just pen and paper is the NSA.'s DIANA system. On the right-hand side are many different substitution alphabets, and on the left-hand side is a random string of letters. Each successive letter on the left indicates which substitution alphabet should be used for each successive character of the message.

NSA DIANA one-time pad:

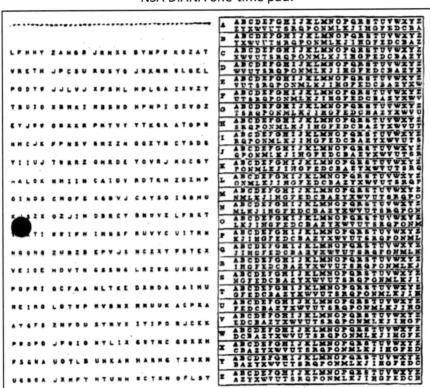

If you look closely at this one-time pad, you should see that it specifies that the first letter of the plaintext should be enciphered using the "L" substitution alphabet, the second letter of plaintext using "F" substitution alphabet, the third letter using the "N" substitution alphabet, the fourth letter also using the "N" substitution alphabet, the fifth using "Y" substitution alphabet, and so on.

Let's demonstrate how the above one-time pad could be used to encipher a message (for the purposes of this example, let us assume the plaintext message is "SEND HELP"):

- The one-time pad tells to use the "L" substitution alphabet (1) for the first letter of plaintext (which is "S"). We look at the "L" substitution alphabet (2) and locate "S" in the top row (3). The ciphertext equivalent is below: it is a "W".

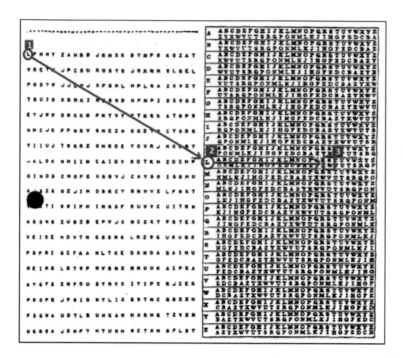

- The one-time pad tells to use the "F" substitution alphabet (1) for the second letter of plaintext (which is "E"). We look at the "F" substitution alphabet (2) and locate "E" in the top row (3). The ciphertext equivalent is below: it is a "Q".

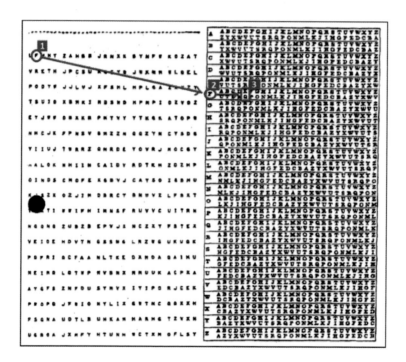

- The one-time pad tells to use the "N" substitution alphabet for the third letter of plaintext (which is "N"). We look at the "N" substitution alphabet and locate "N" in the top row. The ciphertext equivalent is below: it is a "Z".
- The one-time pad tells to use the "N" substitution alphabet for the fourth letter of plaintext (which is "D"). We look at the "N" substitution alphabet and locate "D" in the top row. The ciphertext equivalent is below: it is a "J".

- The one-time pad tells to use the "Y" substitution alphabet for the fifth letter of plaintext (which is "H"). We look at the "Y" substitution alphabet and locate "H" in the top row. The ciphertext equivalent is below: it is a "U".
- The one-time pad tells to use the "Z" substitution alphabet for the sixth letter of plaintext (which is "E"). We look at the "Z" substitution alphabet and locate "E" in the top row. The ciphertext equivalent is below: it is a "W".
- The one-time pad tells to use the "A" substitution alphabet for the seventh letter of plaintext (which is "L"). We look at the "A" substitution alphabet and locate "L" in the top row. The ciphertext equivalent is below: it is an "O".
- The one-time pad tells to use the "M" substitution alphabet for the eighth letter of plaintext (which is "P"). We look at the "M" substitution alphabet and locate "P" in the top row. The ciphertext equivalent is below: it is a "Y".
- Thus, the entire message enciphered (removing spaces and arranging characters into groups of five) would read "WQZJU WOY".

Deciphering messages requires that the recipient have the same one-time pad as the transmitter. The process followed to decipher the message is almost exactly the same as that to encipher it, but the difference is that instead of using the substitution alphabets to convert plaintext to ciphertext, the reverse is done, ciphertext is converted to plaintext.

Let's demonstrate how the recipient would decipher an enciphered message, in this case "WQZJU WOY":

- The one-time pad tells to use the "L" substitution alphabet (1) for the first letter of ciphertext (which is "W"). We look at the "L" substitution alphabet (2) and locate "W" in the bottom row (3). The plaintext equivalent is above: it is a "S".

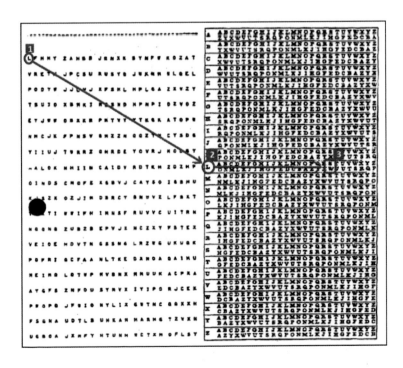

- The one-time pad tells to use the "F" substitution alphabet (1) for the second letter of ciphertext (which is "Q"). We look at the "F" substitution alphabet (2) and locate "Q" in the bottom row (3). The plaintext equivalent is above: it is a "E".

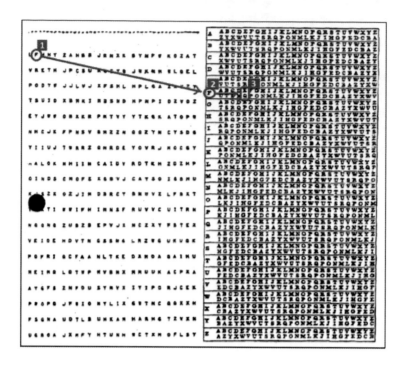

- The one-time pad tells to use the "N" substitution alphabet for the third letter of ciphertext (which is "Z"). We look at the "N" substitution alphabet and locate "Z" in the bottom row. The plaintext equivalent is above: it is a "N".
- The one-time pad tells to use the "N" substitution alphabet for the fourth letter of ciphertext (which is "J"). We look at the "N" substitution alphabet and locate "J" in the bottom row. The plaintext equivalent is above: it is a "D".
- The one-time pad tells to use the "Y" substitution alphabet for the fifth letter of ciphertext (which is "U"). We look at the "Y" substitution alphabet and locate "U" in the bottom row. The plaintext equivalent is above: it is a "H".
- The one-time pad tells to use the "Z" substitution alphabet for the sixth letter of ciphertext (which is "W"). We look at the "Z" substitution alphabet and locate "W" in the bottom row. The plaintext equivalent is above: it is a "E".
- The one-time pad tells to use the "A" substitution alphabet for the seventh letter of ciphertext (which is "O"). We look at the "A" substitution alphabet and locate "O" in the bottom row. The plaintext equivalent is above: it is an "L".
- The one-time pad tells to use the "M" substitution alphabet for the eighth letter of ciphertext (which is "Y"). We look at the "M" substitution alphabet and locate "Y" in the bottom row. The plaintext equivalent is above: it is a "P".
- Thus, the entire message deciphered (inserting spaces in appropriate places) would read "SEND HELP".

NSA MEDEA one-time pad. The first character of a message would be enciphered (and deciphered) using substitution alphabet labelled 01, the second using substitution alphabet 02, and so on:

Difficulties of Implementing a Perfect Cipher

While a one-time pad offers perfect secrecy, this is only true if the cipher is implemented and used properly. In real world situations, this does **not** always happen, and as a result supposedly perfect ciphers have been broken.

In this section, we will discuss some of the requirements needed to implement a perfect cipher, the difficulties of meeting these requirements, and how hostile cryptanalysts can exploit any failures to meet the requirements.

Protecting the Key

As we have already discussed, the key for a one-time pad must contain at least as many characters as the message to be enciphered. Moreover, the key needs to be made available to both the transmitter and the recipient of the message. There is obviously a potential practical difficulty in distributing the key. For all but the very shortest messages, the key will be too long for a person to memorize, especially since the key needs to be completely random. This therefore means the key needs to be committed to paper or stored in electronic form (such on an optical disk, a computer's hard-disk, or a USB memory stick), etc., and this item needs to be made available to both the transmitter and recipient.

If the key is intercepted or captured by an attacker at any point, and recognized as being a key, this allows the attacker to decipher the message sent using that key, so it is obviously critical to protect the key. Moreover, the problem of protecting the key does **not** end after a message has been sent and received, as the key must be also disposed of securely. This is because an attacker could potentially intercept enciphered messages, obtain the key later, and decipher the messages after the fact. Completing disposing of data in electronic storage is **not** necessarily easy, as data may still be recoverable even after it has electronically deleted, and even physically smashing or breaking a device can still leave part of the key potentially recoverable.

Not Reusing the Key

Any reuse of the key compromises the security of a one-time pad, so ensuring that this does **not** happen is crucial to protecting the cipher. Supposedly secure one-time pad systems can and have been broken because of operators making this mistake:

- The USSR used to typists to generate one-time pads for use by their secret agents and their controllers. During the German invasion of the USSR during World War II, there seems to have a lot of pressure to quickly produce a large volume of one-time pads. Asa result, the same keys were used more than once on some one-time pads. This provided an opening for US cryptanalysts, which allowed them to decipher some enciphered Soviet messages. Several thousand Soviet messages were deciphered in a project known as Venona. Venona revealed many secrets including Soviet espionage against the Manhattan Project and existence of the Cambridge Five spy ring in the United Kingdom.
- In 1945, the United States discovered that the USSR was using the same one-time pads for transmissions from Canberra (in Australia) to Moscow as for transmissions from Washington DC to Moscow. This combined with the fact that the plaintext for some of the Canberra-Moscow messages was known to include some British government documents, allowed US cryptanalysts to decipher a number of Soviet messages.

Although it was **not** revealed at the time, intelligence from Venona provided important information about the espionage activities of Soviet spies Julius and Ethel Rosenberg:

Randomness in the Key

One-time pads are only truly secure if the keys are truly random, this is because if there is any mathematical pattern in the key, a cryptanalyst may be able to discover and exploit it.

- As we have seen with Enigma (when operators were choosing message keys), humans are very poor at generating randomness and tend to have predictable patterns of behavior.
- Computers can also be poor at generating random data. For example, most programming languages have a feature for generating "random" numbers, but such numbers are usually only **pseudorandom** (they appear random on casual inspection but are in fact generated by a deterministic mathematical procedure). If an attacker knows or reverse engineers the procedure, he can recreate the entire sequence of "random" numbers. As a result of this, great care must be taken when designing one-time pad systems to only use truly random (**cryptographically secure**) sources of randomness.

The Equipment Used Must Be Secure

All the equipment used during the initial creation of the one-time pad, and during the encipherment and decipherment stages must be secure. If the equipment "leaks" information, an attacker may be able to use that to obtain the key or the plaintext directly.

- For example, if one-time pads are prepared manually by a typist (as was done by the Soviets in the 1940s), an attacker might try to obtain the typewriter ribbons.
- Electronic equipment has been known to produce unintended electromagnetic emissions. An attacker may be able to monitor these emissions and from them obtain the key or the plaintext directly. For example, during World War II, Bell Labs discovered that an electromechanical device used by the US with one-time ciphers produced exactly these types of emissions. Subsequently, the US National Security Agency set up a program named TEMPEST (Telecommunications Electronics Materials Protected from Emanating Spurious Transmissions) to shield its own equipment and stop unintended emissions of this type, and to spy on emissions made by foreign equipment.

The type 131B2 mixer was used by the US to encipher and decipher teletypewriter transmissions using the Vernam Cipher XOR method. Bell Labs discovered that the plaintext could be read by an attacker because of the machine's unintended electromagnetic emissions:

Lorenz Cipher

The Lorenz SZ40, SZ42a and SZ42b were cipher machines used by the German Army during World War II. "SZ" stood for *Schlüssel-Zusatz* which means "cipher attachment", and this reflects the fact the ciphers machines were attachments that fitted to standard teleprinters.

The Germans began using the early SZ40 machines from June 1941 onwards, and the improved SZ42 machines from mid-1942 onwards. The system was used for communications between the German High Command in Wünsdorf near Berlin to the various Army Commands in the field. Due to high-level information on this network, it represented an extremely valuable target for Allied cryptanalysts.

Lorenz SZ42 cipher machine with covers removed:

The Lorenz machines worked much like the machine that Gilbert Vernam had patented in 1919, but there were two important differences:

- Signals were transmitted by radio (and using a coding system called Radioteletype rather than Morse code) rather than by telegraph landline.
- The cipher key did **not** come from punched holes in a paper tape. Instead there were rotor wheels with moveable pins around the rims. The rotor wheels moved in a complicated pattern after each character, and the positions of the pins determined the key to XOR with the current character of plaintext (when enciphering) or ciphertext (when deciphering). The earliest Lorenz machines had ten rotors, but later machines had twelve rotors as well as

other enhancements designed to make it harder for an attacker to discover a pattern in the keys.

Close-up of some of the wheels in the Lorenz SZ42. The position of the wheels and the pins on them determined the key XORed with the current plaintext character:

The Germans set up pairs of transmitting and receiving Lorenz machines at each end of a link (a total four machines per link). Each pair of sending and receiving machines needed to use the same sequence of keys, which required that the machines were configured identically including the initial positions of the rotors. Initially, this was done by the operator preceding each message with an unenciphered 12-letter code (**indicator**). From October 1942, the system was changed, so that the operator instead sent unenciphered "QEP" followed by a 2-digit code, the code referencing a list of settings in a book (called the **QEP book**). Each listing in the QEP book was supposed to be used only once (but sometimes the Germans reused listings) and new books were issued periodically.

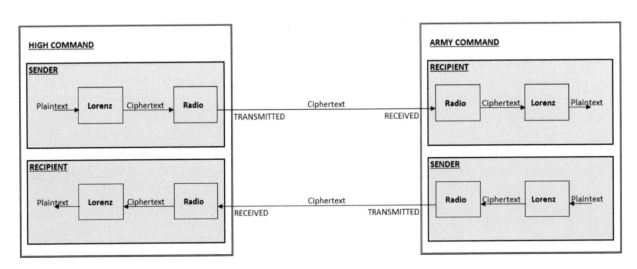

Cryptanalysis of the Lorenz Cipher

German Lorenz radio transmissions were picked up by the British signals intelligence stations at Knockholt in Kent and at Denmark Hill in Camberwell, London. The content of the signals was recorded and then passed on to GC&CS at Bletchley Park for analysis. British cryptanalysts referred to the enciphered radio traffic as *Fish*, deduced that a cryptographic machine must be involved, and referred to the combination of the machine and its traffic as *Tunny* (in reference to tunafish).

The first major break that British cryptanalysts received was on August 30th, 1941. The Germans transmitted a message from Athens to Vienna, but the message was **not** received correctly at the other end. The recipient sent an unenciphered request back to Athens explaining the problem and asking for the message to be resent. Because this request was in the clear, the British knew exactly what was happening. The operator then made a second mistake: he resent the message without changing the key settings. This error was compounded by the fact that during the retransmission the operator slightly changed the message, for example using some abbreviations instead of full spelling out words.

At Bletchley Park, John Tiltman (who we previously encountered in Chapter 8) was able to decipher both plaintexts of from the August 30th, 1941 messages, and the sequences of keys (**keystream**). However, even after three months' work, he was **not** able to figure out how the keystream was generated as it appeared to be random.

In late 1941, the task of discovering a pattern in the keystream was passed on to the mathematician, William Thomas "Bill" Tutte (May 14th, 1917 to May 2nd, 2002). Tutte eventually discovered a repetition within the keystream that occurred every 41 characters. Despite having never seen a Lorenz machine, Tutte and his colleagues were able to deduce its entire logical structure by early 1942.

Once the British cryptanalysts understood how the cipher worked, they set about automating the process of deciphering as many German messages as possible. To this end, they developed several machines, including:

- British Tunny Machine – The first machine created was the British Tunny Machine. This was machine was intended to replicate the functions of the SZ cipher machines after its settings had been determined.
- Robinsons – The Robinsons (also sometimes called Heath Robinsons) were named after the cartoonist W. Heath Robinson (May 31st, 1872 to September 13th, 1944) who had become famous for his humorous illustrations of elaborate machines designed to perform simple tasks. The Robinson machines were used to determine the settings of some of the wheels in the SZ cipher machines.
- Colossus – Colossus was a computer designed to perform logical and counting operations that were useful in deciphering messages in the Lorenz cipher. The prototype machine (Colossus Mark 1) was completed in late 1943 and put to work at Bletchley Park in early 1944. The first production machine (Colossus Mark 2) was completed and working on June 1st, 1944. Ten Colossus Mark 2 computers were in use by the end of World War II, with an eleventh under construction. Although Colossus did **not** have the ability to store programs (programs were entered by switches and plug connections), it is today regarded as the first programmable electronic digital computer.

A Colossus computer at Bletchley Park during World War II:

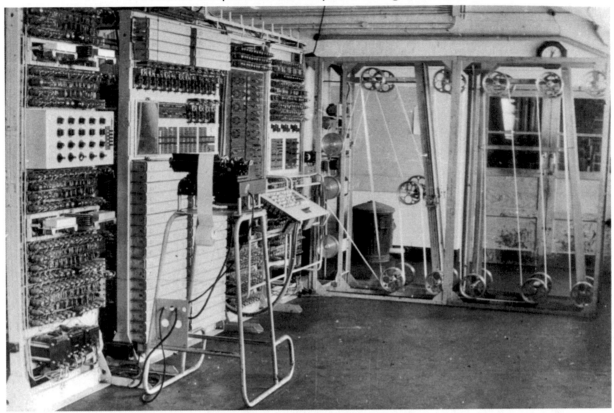

Colossus Mark 2 computer being operated by WRENs:

Chapter 10: Codewords

A **codeword** (also called a **codename** or **cryptonym**) is a word or phrase used to refer to another word, or a location, name, operation, person or project. Sometimes the purpose of using a codeword is to act as a cipher:

- If a message is broadcast unenciphered, providing meaning of the codeword is kept secret, an opponent may **not** be able to deduce the complete meaning of a message.
- Codewords maybe used in the plaintext version of a message, before a message is enciphered and transmitted. In such a case, the message is said to be **superenciphered** since it contains a cipher within a cipher. Superenciphering means that even if an opponent's cryptanalysts are able to decipher a message, they still may **not** be able to deduce the entire meaning of the message.

Some examples of well-known codewords used historically include:

- Codewords used for Allied military operations in World War II such as *Dynamo* (the Dunkirk evacuation), *Compass* (the Western Desert campaign), *Torch* (landings in North Africa), *Husky* (invasion of Sicily), *Overlord* (D-Day landings in Normandy) and so on.
- Western powers have continued to use codewords to identify their military operations since World War II, such as *Corporate* (the British operation to recapture the Falkland Islands in 1982), *Desert Storm* (the US led operation to liberate Kuwait from Iraqi occupation in 1991), and *Neptune Spear* (the 2011 US military raid on Osama bin Laden's compound in Pakistan).
- The Germans also used codewords to identify their World War II operations such *Weserübung* (the invasion of Denmark and Norway), *Seelöwe* (the planned invasion of the UK), *Rheinübung* (the sortie of *Bismark* and *Prinz Eugen*), *Barbarossa* (the invasion of Russia) and *Wacht am Rhein* (the Battle of the Bulge offensive).
- During World War II, Allied forces found the Japanese naming system for their aircraft confusing. This is because the Japanese had two names for each aircraft and used a number based on the year that aircraft was introduced (so the same number could apply to one aircraft). In 1942, Captain Frank T. McCoy, an officer in the US Army Air Forces introduced a system of reporting names that caught on quickly among Allied forces. Fighters were given boys' names and bombers were given girls' names. Later the system was extended to include other types of aircraft: training aircraft were named after trees, gliders were named after birds, transports were given girls' names beginning with the letter "T", single engine reconnaissance aircraft were given men's names, and multi-engine reconnaissance aircraft were given women's names.
- After World War II, the United States, Britain, Canada, Australia and New Zealand created the Air Standards Co-ordinating Committee (ASCC) to give reporting names to Soviet and Chinese aircraft. This system was later extended to include all NATO allies and now covers missiles and rockets as well as aircraft. Some well-known examples include *Fishbed* for the MiG-21, *Fencer* of the MiG-23, *Foxbat* for the MiG-25, *Fulcrum* for the MiG-29, *Badger* for the Tu-95 and *Blackjack* for the Tu-160.
- The US Central Intelligence Agency (CIA) is known to have used cryptonyms (some codewords and some two-character digraphs) to refer to places, people or organizations. Some probable examples that have been used are *AE* for the USSR, *AM* for Cuba, *BE* for Poland, *DB* for Iraq, *AMQUACK* for Che Guevara, and *KUBARK* for the CIA Headquarters in Langley, Virginia.
- Many companies have used codewords to identify development projects. For example, Microsoft have used names like *Cairo, Chicago, Daytona, Memphis, Longhorn* and *Cairo* to identify various versions of Microsoft Windows when under development. Similarly, Apple

has used names such as *Copland*, *Gershwin*, *Snow Leopard* and *Lion* to refer to various versions of the macOS operation system.

- Airports, hospitals and business organizations may use codes to discretely announce emergencies to staff without causing a panic. For example, many businesses use "Could Inspector Sands please report to…" to indicate a fire, and similarly many hospitals use "Paging Doctor Firestone to…". Likewise, airports may use "Bravo" to report a security breach and some cruise ships use "Oscar" to report a man overboard.

Soviet and Russian aircraft like this Tupolev Tu-95RT are generally best known in the West by their reporting codename (in this case *Bear D*):

One-time Code

A **one-time code** is a codeword or phrase that is intended to convey some prearranged message simply by its presence. Sometimes codewords can even be inserted as an apparently innocent part of a normal conversation, so that adversaries listening in do **not** become aware of the presence of the one-time code.

Some famous examples one-time codes include:

- "Over all of Spain, the sky is clear" was the one-time code included a radio broadcast that instructed Spanish Nationalist forces to begin a military uprising in 1936.
- "Climb Mount Niitaka" was the one-time code sent to Japanese aircraft to begin their attack on Pearl Harbor in 1941.
- "Superfuze" was broadcast by a British Avro Vulcan bomber to indicate it had successfully attacked Port Stanley Airport's runway in 1982.

Nomenclator

Nomenclator ciphers were a common type of cipher that was widely used in diplomatic correspondence from about the early fifteenth century through until the late eighteenth century. Nomenclator is named after the public official who announced the names of visiting dignitaries and these types of ciphers original were based around code books that assigned a symbol or code number to the names of important people. Later variants of nomenclator were extended with additional symbols or numbers corresponding to words, names of places, and syllables and letters.

Additionally, sometimes the same person, place, syllable or letter could be assigned the several different numbers in order to make cryptanalysis harder.

The codebook for a 17th century French nomenclator:

The Battle of Midway

One of the most famous incidents involving a codeword occurred in the prelude to the Battle of Midway (June 4th, 1942 to June 7th, 1942) during World War II. It has been argued that cryptanalysis had a decisive effect on the outcome of the battle. This is especially significant as the battle is regarded as one of the turning points of World War II.

The Japanese Navy used a cipher that the Allies dubbed JN-25. British cryptanalysts John Tiltman and Alan Turing had already figured out ("solved") the structure of JN-25 in 1941, but even so could only read about 20% of JN-25 traffic as it contained many codewords with meanings that were **not** understood. Despite two revisions to the JN-25 cipher, which Allied cryptanalysts dubbed JN-25a and JN-25b, cryptanalysts in the US Navy's Combat Intelligence Unit (also known as Station Hypo) soon become extremely good at rapidly intercepting and deciphering Japanese radio traffic in JN-25b.

In May 1941, Station Hypo discovered that Japanese Admiral Isoroku Yamamoto was planning a major attack at a location in the Pacific that was simply referred to by the initials *AF*. Lieutenant

Commander Joseph Rochefort (May 12th, 1900 to July 20th, 1976), who was in charge of Station Hypo, already suspected that *AF* referred to the Midway Atoll in the Central Pacific, but he needed confirmatory evidence. One of the Station Hypo staff, Wilfred J. "Jasper" Holmes (April 4th, 1900 to January 7th, 1986) suggested a clever ruse to obtain this evidence. A message was sent by undersea cable to Midway instructing the US personnel on the island to radio back that the water purification system on the island had broken down. The ruse worked: just two days a Japanese message in JN-25b reported that freshwater was running out at *AF*.

Joseph Rochefort:

There was still the problem of knowing when the Japanese attack was planned for. The problem was that the date-time data in JN-25b was superenciphered in a second cipher. A prodigious effort by Rochefort and his group which involved deciphering hundreds of Japanese messages per day, eventually yielded this information in late May 1942.

Intercept and translation of Japanese message in the JN-25 cipher:

Armed with knowledge of the Japanese plan's Admiral Chester W. Nimitz (February 24th, 1885 to February 20th, 1966) was able to prepare a trap for them. Three US aircraft carriers, the *USS Enterprise*, the *USS Hornet* and the *USS Yorktown*, assembled 350 miles (560 km) northeast of

Midway at a location dubbed "Point Luck". Moreover, armed with knowledge of the Japanese Navy's plans, the US Navy was able to win a major victory in the Battle of Midway – a victory which is widely considered to be the turning point of World War II in the Pacific.

Douglas TBD-1 Devastators preparing to take off from the *USS Enterprise* during the Battle of Midway:

Chapter 11: Book Ciphers

A **book cipher** is a cipher which uses some aspect of a book or other document as an essential part of the cipher. It is normally required that both sender and recipient have access to identical copies of the book – **not** just the same book, but the same edition. It is also normally essential that the identity of the book be kept secret from adversaries, as if it becomes known, cryptanalysts can break the cipher relatively easily.

A practical difficulty of book ciphers is that agents need to be keep the chosen book with them, which can be difficult under field conditions. Moreover, in the case of an undercover agent, the possession of a book should **not** be one that attracts suspicion – it should be a book that fits in with the agent's cover story. Some of the books that are known to have been used include various editions of the Bible, dictionaries and even industrial almanacs.

Book Word Substitution Ciphers

In a **book word substitution cipher** (sometimes called an **Ottendorf cipher**), the ciphertext encodes the locations of word within the chosen book. For example, using A=1, B=2, C=3, D=4, a ciphertext fragment such as "MGB" could be used to indicate the numbers 13, 7 and 2, meaning page 13, line 7, 2nd word, and with many such fragments an entire message could be encoded. Likewise, if using the Bible, chapter and verse references could be used to locate the word.

One obvious problem with this type of cipher is that the book may **not** contain all the words that need to be enciphered. Using a dictionary would avoid this problem, and this was the approach used by George Scovell (March 21st, 1774 to January 17th, 1861) during the Peninsular War. Scovell used a combination of the page number, a letter to indicate which column in the page, and a second number to indicate the entry in the column.

Book Letter Substitution Ciphers

An alternative to using the ciphertext to encode the locations of words within a book is to encode the locations of individual letters within the book. For example, using A=1, B=2, C=3, D=4, a ciphertext fragment such as "MGB" could be used to indicate the numbers 13, 7 and 2, meaning the first letter of page 13, line 7, 2nd word. Alternatively, a fragment such as "MGBD" could be used to indicate the numbers 13, 7,2 and 4 meaning the 4th character of page 13, line 7, 2nd word.

Running Key Ciphers

Another method of using a book in cryptography is to use the text of a book (or part of the text) as a key for a more conventional cipher. For example, we saw in Chapter 7 that the weakness of the Vigenère and Beaufort ciphers was that the key was relatively short and is repeated at regular intervals. Using text from a book, in what is known as a **running key cipher**, allows the use of a key which is extremely long (as long as the message) and does **not** repeat.

The way a running key cipher works is that the ciphertext is preceded by short prefix indicating where in the book the key begins. For example, using A=1, B=2, C=3, D=4, the prefix "MGB" would indicate the key begins on page 13, line 7, at the 2nd word. The text of the book is then used as the key.

Example of a running key cipher using a Bible verse as the key:

There are two main weaknesses in running key ciphers:

- The key text itself is **not** random but contains normal words in the chosen language. This means an adversary can attack the ciphertext using similar techniques to those used against autokey ciphers (see Chapter 7).
- Although it may seem that there are many possible books and starting positions that could be used, the number is **not** so large as to be beyond computerized search. For example, if there were 100,000,000 possible key texts with an average of 10,000 possible starting positions per text, that is just 1,000,000,000,000 ($10^{12} \approx 2^{40}$) possible combinations. This might sound like a lot of combinations, but nowadays computers are capable of checking all these combinations in a relatively short time.

Chapter 12: Computer Cryptography

Today we live in an age of digital computers that can perform mathematical and logical operations at incredible speeds. Computers can also access and make use of massive databases of information such as the text of all common books published in English or another language. Moreover, computers are getting faster and more capable all the time.

The advent of computers has fundamentally changed cryptography – so much so, that anything prior to the advent of computers is generally called **classical cryptography**.

- We have seen in Chapter 8 (Enigma) and Chapter 9 (Lorenz) that data processing by bombes and early computers (Colossus) allowed cryptanalysts to decipher even the most complicated classical ciphers
- In Chapter 11, when talking about book ciphers, we discovered that computers could perform the kind of comprehensive search against millions of texts that would be unimaginable to a human.

The upshot of this, is that in the age of computers, cryptanalysis has become so powerful that new types of ciphers have had to be devised. These ciphers use computers' data processing capabilities, but they are also based on mathematics and computer science. Modern ciphers are designed to either be informationally-theoretically secure (unbreakable even with unlimited computing power) such as the one-time pad, or when that is **not** practical, to be **computationally hard** (difficult for a computer to solve in a reasonable time frame). One issue is that our understanding of what is computationally hard has changed over time, and will probably continue to change, as computers improve and as we make new mathematical discoveries.

An example of a computationally hard problem today is integer factorization of large semiprimes. Multiplying two prime numbers (positive whole numbers that are divisible only by themselves and one) to produce a semiprime (a number divisible only by itself, one, and two prime numbers) requires much less computational effort than starting with a semiprime and finding its two prime factors. It is a lot easier to calculate $54,217 \times 83,101$ than it is to start with $4,505,486,917$ and find its two prime factors. Modern computers can of course handle the computation required to factorize a 10-digit semiprime easily, so we need to use a much larger semiprimes, but the same principle applies. There are however potential pitfalls that cryptographers need to be aware of:

- Computers are generally improving in speed and power. As a result, it is now possible to factorize semiprimes that were once infeasible to factorize, so larger and larger semiprimes are needed. This trend is expected to continue. For example, a 129-digit semiprime was considered secure in 1977, but today (as of early 2020) use of up to 617 digits is recommended (see "The Magic Words are Squeamish Ossifrage" in Chapter 14).
- For many supposed computationally hard problems (including factorizing large semiprimes) it suspected, but **not** proven, that no efficient algorithm exists that would drastically reduce the time to solve the problem. It therefore remains possible that a breakthrough in mathematics or computer science could render obsolete those ciphers which depend on that problem.

Symmetric-Key Cryptography

Symmetric-key cryptography can be considered the computerized equivalent of classical cryptography. The same key is used for both enciphering (generally called encrypting in this context) the plaintext into ciphertext, and for deciphering (generally called decrypting) the ciphertext back into plaintext. The key is therefore a **shared key**: it must be shared between the transmitter of a message and the recipient(s). It is also a **shared secret**, because if the key is discovered or released to third parties, then they too can read the ciphertext.

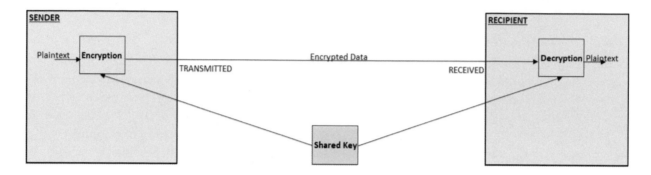

The big disadvantage of symmetric-key ciphers is the shared secret. It means that a way must be found to securely distribute the key to those parties that need it, and only those parties. Moreover, the key must be kept secret **not** only during distribution, but by multiple parties when in use and after use.

In terms of implementation, symmetric-key ciphers can be implemented as stream ciphers or block ciphers:

- A **stream cipher** enciphers a continuous stream of bits or characters.
- A **block cipher** enciphers blocks of data (each block usually comprising several characters or over 100 bits).

Some examples of popular symmetric-key cipher algorithms including AES (the Advanced Encryption Standard) which is also known as Rijndael, DES (Data Encryption Standard), Triple DES (3DES or TDES), Blowfish, CAST5, IDEA (International Data Encryption Algorithm), Kuznyechik, RC4, Serpent, Skipjack and Twofish.

Public-Key Cryptography

Public-key cryptography (also known as **asymmetric cryptography**) is an innovation in cryptography that was first introduced in the computer age. The idea is that anybody can create encrypted messages intended for a particular recipient, but only the intended recipient can decrypt these messages.

This is possible because each intended recipient has two keys to the cipher keys:

- A **public key** that is used to encrypt data. The public key does **not** need to be kept secret and can be freely shared. A person who wants to receive messages, can therefore publish their public key to as many others as they want, as it allows these people to send them encrypted messages.
- A **private key** that is used to decrypt data. The private key is **never** shared and is kept secret.

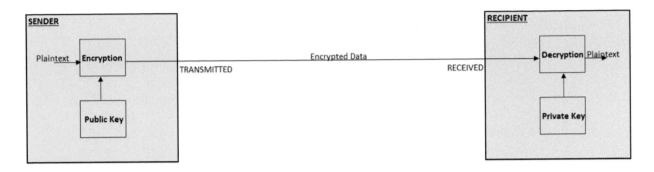

The first public description of public-key cryptography was in a 1976 paper called *New Directions in Cryptography* written by Bailey Whitfield "Whit" Diffie and Martin Edward Hellman. While the Diffie and Hellman paper showed that public-key cryptography was possible, it did **not** provide all the details necessary for a practical public-key encryption system. The first practical implementation was created by Ronald Rivest, Adi Shamir, and Len Adleman, and has since become known as the RSA algorithm. Since then other implementations of public-key cryptography have been created by others and public-key cryptography has come to form the basis of many internet and software standards including GPG (GNU Privacy Guard), PGP (Pretty Good Privacy), S/MIME (Secure/Multipurpose Internet Mail Extensions) and TLS (Transport Layer Security).

In 1997, it emerged that a British intelligence organization, Government Communication Headquarters (GCHQ) anticipated many of the developments in public-key cryptography long before the academic community. While working at GCHQ in 1970, James H. Ellis (September 25th, 1924 to November 25th, 1997) wrote a paper entitled *The Possibility of Secure Non-Secret Digital Encryption*, but his discovery was kept secret.

Cryptographic Hashes and Digital Signatures

Cryptographic hashes are algorithms that take in input data of any length (potentially millions of bits or more) and generate a short **hash** (typically a few hundred bits) based on the content of the data.

The algorithms used in cryptographic hashing are published. The idea is that when somebody receives a copy of the data, they can recalculate the hash to see if it the same as it was originally (indicating the data is unchanged) or whether it is different (indicating the data has changed). Thus the cryptographic hash acts as a kind of **digital signature**.

The ideal hashing algorithm is sensitive to even the smallest changes to the data, so that changing even a single bit of the data will result in a different hash. Moreover, it should be **computationally infeasible** for an adversary to create data that matches a desired hash value, as this would allow the possibility of forgery.

Some well-known examples of hash functions include MD4, MD5, SHA-1, SHA-2 and SHA-3. MD4 and MD5 are however very insecure, as even home computers can create data that matches a desired hash value. Possible attacks have also been identified against SHA-1 and SHA-2.

Chapter 13: Steganography and Hidden Messages

Steganography is the art of concealing one message (or file, data, image, video etc.) as hidden information within another message (or file, data, image, video, etc.). Very often the visible message may appear to be something entirely different from the hidden message. For example, a steganographic message to a secret agent might outwardly appear to be a shopping list or a love letter. The term steganography was coined by Johannes Trithemius (who we encountered in Chapter 7) as title of his 1499 book, *Steganographia*, which was a treatise on cryptography and steganography, but outwardly appeared to be a book about magic.

The Ancient Greek historian Herodotus (c. 484 BC to c. 425 BC) gives the earliest-known examples of steganography in his book, *The Histories*, which was written in about 440 BC. In one story he recounts Histiaeus, the ruler of the Greek city of Miletus in Asia Minor, sent a message to a vassal by shaving the head of a servant, marking the message on the servant's scalp, and after the hair had grown back, sending the servant to deliver the message. In another story, Herodotus says that Demaratus, a king of Sparta, sent a hidden message concealed within a wax tablet by writing on the message on the wooden backing material, before covering the backing with wax.

Some other historical examples of steganographic messaging include:
- Special or invisible inks have been used many times. For example, Giambattista della Porta, who also invented the first polygraphic cipher (see Chapter 6), is said to have provided a method to some of his friends who were imprisoned during the Spanish Inquisition. Della Porta used alum and plant mixtures to write on eggshells and then boiled the eggs. The ink on the shell was washed away when the egg was boiled, but some would have already penetrated the semi-porous eggshell, and the secret message could be revealed by shelling the egg.
- Prisoners have used Polybius Squares (see Chapter 1) as the basis for tapping audible codes.
- Messages in Morse code have been tied as knots on yarn or knitted into clothing,
- Messages have been written on envelopes in the area covered by the postage stamp.
- Spies used cameras to create **microdots** (text or images greatly reduced in size to the size of a dot) which were then embedded in letters or postcards.
- Captured US airmen blinked messages in Morse code during the Vietnam War.
- American prisoners in North Korean captivity signaled in sign language or made obscene gestures to their guards (to indicate that they were **not** willing guests of North Korea).

Microdot camera:

Null Ciphers

One of the most common ways to conceal a message within text is a **null cipher** (also known as a **concealment cipher**). In this case, the secret message (the plaintext) is concealed according to a predefined set of rules within a longer innocuous-looking message (the **covertext**). The covertext is then published or sent to the intended recipient, who knowing the rules, can extract the secret message.

For example:

- Consider the message "Let me be clear. It's unfair that only you have spare time. I think holidays are an issue that we should discuss. Let's be honest and open. Think it over please! You know I'm right."
- This message might appear to be a person demanding more breaks or time away from work, but by looking at the first letter of every third word, another message can be revealed within: "Let me **be** clear. It's **un**fair that only **y**ou have spare **t**ime. I think **h**olidays are an **i**ssue that we **s**hould discuss. Let's **be** honest and **o**pen. Think it **o**ver please! You **k**now I'm right."
- Did you see it? The secret message is "buy this book".

Another famous example was concealed in a press cable by the Germans during World War I:

- The cable read: "President's embargo ruling should have immediate notice. Grave situation affecting international law. Statement foreshadows ruin of many neutrals. Yellow journals unifying national excitement immensely."
- Extracting the first letter of each word reveals the secret message: "Pershing sails from NY June I".

Null ciphers may also be used to conceal individual letters within the covertext (as in the above examples), but they can be used to entire words. The Cryptanalysis and Racketeering Unit (CRRU) of the FBI (Federal Bureau of Investigation) discovered one such example in an apparently innocent message sent by a prison inmate:

SALUDOS LOVED ONE

SO TODAY I HEARD FROM UNCLE MOE OVER THE PHONE. HE TOLD ME THAT YOU AND ME GO THE SAME BIRTHDAY. HE SAYS YOUR TIME THERE TESTED YOUR STRENGTH SO STAY POSITIVE AT SUCH TIMES. I'M FOR ALL THAT CLEAN LIVING! METHAMPHETAMINES WAS MY DOWN FALL. THE PROGRAM I'M STARTING THE NINTH IS ONE I HEARD OF A COUPLE WEEKS BEFORE SEPTEMBER THROUGH MY COUNSELOR BARRIOS. BUT MY MEDICAL INSURANCE COVERAGE DENIES THEY COVER IT. I'M USING MY TIME TO CHECK AND IF THE INSURANCE AGENT DENIES STILL MY COVERAGE I'M GETTING TOGETHER PAPERWORK SAYING I TESTED FOR THIS TREATMENT REQUIRED ON THE CHILD CUSTODY. THE NINTH WILL MEAN I HAVE TESTED MY DETERMINATION TO CHANGE. ON THE NEXT FREE WEEKEND THE KIDS ARE COMING, BUT FIRST I GOTTA SHOW CAROLINA I'M STAYING OUT OF TROUBLE WAITING TO GET MYSELF ADMITTED ON THE PROGRAM. THE SUPPORTING PAPERWORK THAT THE FAMILY COURTS GOT WILL ALSO PROVE THERE'S NO REASON NEITHER FOR A WITNESS ON MY CHILDREN'S VISITS. OF COURSE MY BRO HAS HIS MIND MADE UP OF RECENT THAT ALL THIS DRUG USAGE DON'T CONCERN OUR VISITS. I THINK THAT MY KIDS FEEL I NEED THEIR LOVE IF I'M GONNA BE COOL. GUILTY FEELINGS RISE ON ACCOUNT OF THE MISTAKES I COULD WRITEUP. FOR DAYS I'M HERE. HE GOT A GOOD HEART. SHOULD YOU BE HAVING PROBLEMS BE ASSURED THAT WHEN YOU HIT THE STREETS WE'LL BE CONSIDERING YOU...

Reading every fifth word of the covertext reveals the secret message: "TODAY MOE TOLD ME HE TESTED POSITIVE FOR METHAMPHETAMINES THE NINTH OF SEPTEMBER BUT DENIES USING AND DENIES GETTING TESTED ON NINTH. TESTED ON FIRST. I'M WAITING ON PAPERWORK. GOT NO WITNESS OF HIS RECENT USAGE. I FEEL IF GUILTY OF WRITEUP HE SHOULD BE HIT."

In general, the rules used to conceal the letters or words can be as simple or as complicated as needed. They can be based on word or letter positions within the covertext, or the position on the page (for example, the last word of every line), or some other cue. This means there are a lot of options for concealing a message within the covertext, although in almost all cases, the covertext will be significantly longer than the plaintext.

While null ciphers can be effective, the biggest problem with them is the difficulty of producing natural-looking covertext around the plaintext. This can be both time-consuming and difficult, and if the covertext appears unnatural, it can raise suspicion.

Bacon's Cipher

Bacon's cipher, also known as the **Baconian cipher**, is a stenographic method which conceals a message within the presentation of the covertext, rather than in the content of covertext. It was devised in 1605 by Francis Bacon (January 22nd, 1561 to April 9th, 1626), an English philosopher and statesman, who later served as Attorney General of England and Wales, and later still as Lord High Chancellor of England.

Francis Bacon:

Bacon's idea was that it was to create a 5-bit code (he used "a"s and "b"s but using "0"s and "1"s is effectively equivalent) which represented the letters of the alphabet. For example, "aaaaa" might represent "A", "aaaab" might represent "B", "aaaba" might represent C, and so on, with, for example, "babba" representing "Y". Once the secret message had been converted into these codes (for example "BAY" would be encoded to "aaaba aaaab babba"), it would be hidden within the covertext. Every "a" would be expressed by a character in one typeface in the covertext, and every "b" would be expressed by having a character in a second typeface in the covertext. The textual content of the covertext was irrelevant, and the covertext could be on any subject and use any wording, since the true meaning was expressed by the sequence of typefaces rather than anything else.

Francis Bacon's original coding scheme:

(Bacon used the Latin alphabet so "I" and "J" are treated as the same letter, as are "U" and "V")

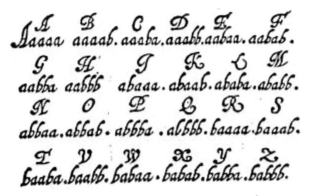

Let's look at an example of using Bacon's cipher:

- The covertext is: Com*e and* see m*e when y*ou vis*it th*e USA.
- In this case each non-italicized letter is an "a", and each italicized letter is a "b".
- The sequence of codes is thus "aaabb aaaaa abbaa aabba aabaa baaaa".
- This corresponds to the plaintext "DANGER".

Grilles

We previously encountered **grilles** (also known as **Cardan grilles**) in Chapter 4. You will recall that they are pieces of paper, card or a similar object with holes in it, through which the letters or words of a message can be written. In Chapter 4, we saw how these can be used in transposition ciphers, but they can also be used for steganographic purposes.

To use a grille for steganography the following steps are followed:

- The person preparing a message (the sender) places his grille over the paper:

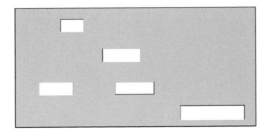

- The sender writes the plaintext secret message through the holes in the grille:

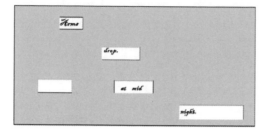

- The sender removes the grille from the paper:

- The sender adds covertext around the plaintext:

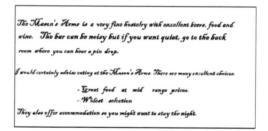

- The message is then sent to the recipient. If the message is intercepted in transit, it will appear to be innocuous.
- When the recipient receives the message, he places his grille over the paper to reveal the secret message:

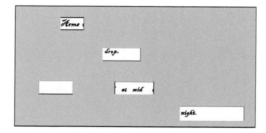

Digital Steganography

Just as the advent of computers and digital technology have had a profound impact on cryptography, so too have they had a similar impact on steganography. This is partly because computers can send and receive vast amounts of data (and there are usually many opportunities to conceal secret information within that data), and partly because the enormous data processing power of computers permit steganographic algorithms that would be impractical to perform manually.

Before we discuss some of these digital stenographic techniques let us first take a moment to understand the **binary** (also known as **base 2** or **radix 2**) number system that computers use internally to represent numbers. Longer and more detailed explanations of binary can be found in my books <u>Binary, Octal and Hexadecimal for Programming & Computer Science</u> and <u>Advanced Binary for Programming & Computer Science: Logical, Bitwise and Arithmetic Operations, and Data Encoding and Representation</u>.

- In the familiar **denary** (also known as **base 10** or **radix 10**) number system, each successive column of a number represents successive powers of 10, and each column contains a digit between 0 and 9 inclusive. The overall value of the number comes from multiplying each digit's value by the column's place value and adding this together. For example, 3947 in denary = $(7 \times 1) + (4 \times 10) + (9 \times 100) + (3 \times 1000)$:

Ten Thousands $(\times 10^4)$ $\times 10000$	Thousands $(\times 10^3)$ $\times 1000$	Hundreds $(\times 10^2)$ $\times 100$	Tens $(\times 10^1)$ $\times 10$	Units $(\times 10^0)$ $\times 1$
	3	9	4	7

- In the binary number system, each successive column of a number represents successive powers of 2, and each column contains a digit (known as a bit) of either 0 or 1. The overall value of the number comes from multiplying each bit's value by the column's place value and adding this together. For example, 11011 in binary would be equivalent to denary 27 because $(1 \times 1) + (1 \times 2) + (0 \times 4) + (1 \times 8) + (1 \times 16) = 27$:

Sixteens $(\times 2^4)$ $\times 16$	Eights $(\times 2^3)$ $\times 8$	Fours $(\times 2^2)$ $\times 4$	Twos $(\times 2^1)$ $\times 2$	Units $(\times 2^0)$ $\times 1$
1	1	0	1	1

- Sometimes a fixed number of bits are allocated to storing a number. For example:
  - If 8 bits are allocated for storage, the number can range from 0 to 255 inclusive.
  - If 12 bits are allocated for storage, the number can range from 0 to 4,095 inclusive.
  - If 16 bits are allocated for storage, the number can range from 0 to 65,535 inclusive.
  - If 24 bits are allocated for storage, the number can range from 0 to 16,777,215 inclusive.
  - If 32 bits are allocated for storage, the number can range from 0 to 4,294,967,295 inclusive.

- The bit that that stores the units value of a binary number is called the **Least Significant Bit (LSB or LSbit)**. Changing the value of Least Significant Bit changes the overall value of the number by plus or minus 1. If the number corresponded to the volume of a sound or the intensity of a color, changing the LSB of an 8-bit number would result in a change of less than 1%, which would be imperceptible by human sense. If more than 8 bits were allocated to storing a sound volume or color intensity, you might be able change several of the least significant bits without it being noticed.

Image Files

As I explain in Chapter 9 of my book <u>Advanced Binary for Programming & Computer Science: Logical, Bitwise and Arithmetic Operations, and Data Encoding and Representation</u>, a common way of representing images within computer memory is as a **bitmap**. A bitmap is a two-dimensional array of small dots known as pixels, and computer memory (or space within a computer file) is used to store the status of each individual pixel.

- In a monochrome bitmap, 1 bit of memory is used per pixel, and this simply stores whether the pixel is on (usually 1) or off (usually 0).
- In a color bitmap display, several bits of memory are used per pixel and in combination these hold a binary number or numbers. In some cases, the numbers store the actual color of the pixel (often as a combination of red, green and blue intensity values). In other cases, these number may store a reference to a table of colors ("**palette**").

Example of displaying an object (a smiley face in this case) using a bitmap display. The enlargement shows the individual pixels that make up the image. The numbers at the bottom show the red, green and blue color intensity values that would be stored for each of the pixels in question:

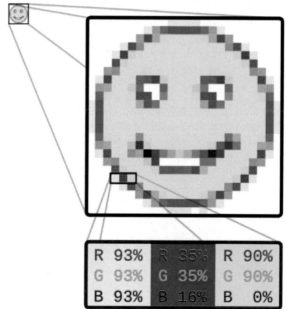

There are many options for adding secret stenographic information to bitmap images. Some of these include:

- Storing information in a few selected pixels of the image. These pixels will **not** have the intended appearance, but if the image is very large and the number of pixels used for this purpose is very small, then this may not be noticeable. One well-known example of this technique is that many color laser-printers automatically add **yellow dots** (yellow pixels) to all printouts, and these dots encode the identifying information about the printer for law enforcement purposes. Many people are **not** aware of these yellow pixels, because yellow is barely visible on white paper, and because around 8,000,000 to 32,000,000 pixels (depending on the resolution of the printer) are typically used when printing a letter-size paper, but only a tiny handful of these pixels are repurposed for stenographic purposes.

Enlargement of part of a laser-printed page showing the yellow dots:

- In a bitmap with a palette, the same color can appear more than once in the palette table. This means each pixel in the bitmap of that color can be represented by two or more different values (since the values in the bitmap reference palette table entries). Hence it is possible to encode information by the sequence of choosing palette entry A or palette entry B for successive pixels of that color without changing any aspect of the appearance of the bitmap.
- In a bitmap with color intensity values stored for each pixel, small changes to the color values (to the least significant bits or some of least significant bits) are unlikely to be perceptible to the human eye. Thus, stenographic information can be placed within individual pixels with only minor and imperceptible changes to the original image. Moreover, the information to be stored can also first be encrypted using a strong cipher (see Chapter 12) before being added to the image, which **not** only improves security but also

makes the stenographic information virtually indistinguishable from random noise. Regardless of whether encryption is used, one thing to be aware is that some image file formats (like JPEG) tend to store color intensity values imperfectly as a means of reducing storage requirements (this is known as **lossy compression**) so are **not** suitable to be used with this type of stenography.

Audio Files

Most audio files consist of a long stream of numbers (or two long streams in the case of a stereo file), with each number corresponding to the amplitude of the sound at any moment in time. There are typically thousands or tens of thousands of numbers for every second of audio. This is known as **pulse code-modulation (PCM)**. If there are enough numbers per second, and the range of the numbers is wide enough, a change to the least significant bit of some or all numbers would probably be imperceptible or nearly so. As with images, enciphering the hidden data before adding to the audio stream would make it virtually indistinguishable from random noise. Also, as with images, there are some audio file formats that use lossy compression, so this type of stenography is **not** suitable in such cases.

Another approach that has been use special software (MetaSynth is the best-known software application of this type) to convert an image into audio. The software converts image in such a way that when the audio is shown on a **spectrogram** (a visual representation of the intensity of different sound frequencies in the audio), the image can be seen. As this technique is widely known, it does **not** provide a secure means of transmitting an image. Some well-known recordings that have used this idea include the song *Windowlicker* by Aphex Twin and the album *Year Zero* by Nine Inch Nails.

Example of a spectrogram (in this case **not** containing a steganographic image). The horizontal axis is time, the vertical axis is frequency, and the brightness of each point in the chart indicates the relative loudness of that frequency at that moment:

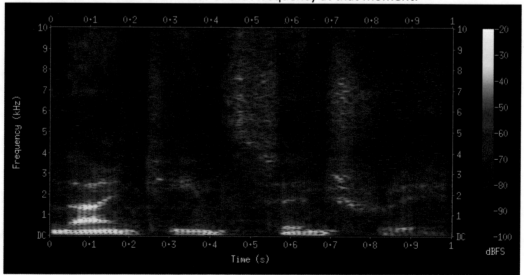

Text and Word Processor Files

Text and word processor files can contain conceal steganographic information. Some of the ways that this can be done include:

- Some character sets contain characters that do **not** print and do **not** affect the display in any way. The presence of such characters, or the relative positions of them within a text file may have a steganographic meaning.
- Some character sets may contain the same character encoded in two or more different ways.
- A text file which contains line breaks could contain an extra space or extra spaces at the end of some lines. The presence or absence of extra spaces (and the number of extra spaces) on each line could have a steganographic meaning.
- Web pages are transmitted over the web as HTML (HyperText Markup Language) files. HTML files are basically ordinary text files but contain special sequences of characters to alter the display or meaning of the text. For example, in HTML text enclosed between a <B> and </B> would display in bold. In HTML, extra spaces and line breaks usually do **not** alter the display or meaning of the content, so can be inserted whenever wanted, and could have a steganographic meaning.
- Word processor files often store **not** only the current revision of a document, but also the change/revision history of the document. It may therefore be possible to insert steganographic meaning in the revision history parts of a word processor file but without changing the current visible/printable version of the document. In some cases, this may be possible from the word processor itself, but in others it may require special software (that understands the word processor's file format) to read and write this data.

Network Communications

When data is transmitted over a computer network, the data is divided up into smaller subdivisions of data (called **packets**) and these are transmitted one at a time over the network. The recipient receives the packets and then reassembles them to reproduce the original data. In many cases, it is **not** required that the packets arrive in order, as each packet contains information about its position within the data.

It is possible to transmit steganographic information without altering the content of any of the packets. Instead the transmitter deliberates varies the delay between packets and uses this to encode secret information. The only problem with this approach is that in some networks (including the internet), the network itself may introduce delays which would disrupt this method of stenographic communication.

Other Examples

There are obviously many other types of data that computers store and process, so there are many ways others to insert steganographic data into computer files. It is **not** possible to list every type of file that a computer might be required to process, but in general any type of redundancy or duplication is likely to provide an opportunity for steganographers. For example:

- Many types of images contain metadata describing the image, for example the type of camera used or the location that a photograph was taken. It may be possible to store concealed information with the metadata.
- Some file formats allow for sections of the file to be ignored by most software. For example, the file may have a logical endpoint and no data after that endpoint is used. In such cases, it is often possible to use special software to read and write these sections, without compromising the normal functionality of the rest of the file.

- Another idea has been to put a steganographic message in blog comments (with the secret message perhaps spread out over several messages and blogs). Since there are thousands of blogs, many of which have been effectively abandoned, there is plenty of opportunity for secretly communicating in this way.

Chapter 14: Famous Codes, Ciphers and Cryptograms – Solved and Unsolved

In this chapter, we will review some famous codes, ciphers and cryptograms. Some of these messages can be deciphered, but in other cases, the meaning of the message is unknown. Some of these messages are even claimed to point to the direction of hidden treasures, lost fortunes and perhaps even the Holy Grail!

Voynich Manuscript

The Voynich manuscript is a handwritten book (codex) written on velum. It is written in an unknown writing system (although it also contains a small amount of Latin script and three German words) and contains many illustrations and diagrams. Some pages are missing, and others are on foldable sheets, but in total there are about 240 pages. The manuscript is bound in goatskin but these are **not** the original bindings: there is evidence that suggests that it was originally bound with a wooden cover with a tanned-leather interior.

The illustrations in different sections of the manuscript relate to various subjects including herbs, recipes, pharmacology, and astronomy or astrology. It has been suggested that manuscript relates to medieval or early modern medicine.

A page of the Voynich manuscript:

The manuscript is named after Wilfrid Voynich (November 12th, 1865 to March 19th, 1930), a Polish book dealer who purchased the manuscript in 1912. The manuscript however seems to be much older (although there is speculation that it may be a hoax), as the vellum has been carbon dated to the early 15th century. Additionally, while the origin of the manuscript is unknown, part of its history has been traced, and the earliest-confirmed owner was Georg Baresch (1585 to 1662), a Czech antique collector.

Sample of text from the Voynich manuscript:

The cryptographic interest in the Voynich manuscript stems from the fact that the text remains undeciphered to this day. While there have been suggestions that the Voynich manuscript is a hoax, some other plausible suggestions include:

- The text is written in a European language using a substitution cipher (see Chapter 3). However, this seems unlikely because the symbol frequencies do **not** resemble any known language, and there do **not** appear to be enough different symbols to encode an alphabet.

- The text is written in a European language using a polyalphabetic cipher (see Chapter 7) where each letter is encoded using a different substitution. However, this also seems unlikely as polyalphabetic ciphers produce ciphertexts where all symbols occur with about equal frequency.
- The text is written using a book cipher (see Chapter 11). It seems possible that the symbols in the manuscript might represent Roman numerals which in turn reference a codebook. However, it would be extremely awkward to write and read such a large book in this type of cipher.
- The text and symbols are largely meaningless, but the meaning is concealed using steganography within small details of the manuscript. These small details might for example the second letter of words, or the length of words, or even the shapes of letters and pen strokes.
- The text is written in a natural or constructed language, using an invented alphabet.

Several people have claimed to have deciphered the Voynich manuscript, but none of these claims have been generally accepted. If you want to try, you can view online scans of the manuscript at https://archive.org/details/TheVoynichManuscript.

Olivier Levasseur

Olivier Levasseur (1688, 1689 or 1690 to July 7th, 1730) was a French pirate nicknamed *La Buse* ("The Buzzard") or *La Bouche* ("The Mouth"). Levasseur was eventually captured by the French government and executed by hanging at Saint-Denis on the Indian Ocean island of Réunion (then known as Île Bourbon). As Levasseur stood on the scaffold prior to his execution, he is said to have a thrown his necklace into the crowd and shouted, "Find my treasure, the one who may understand it!". The necklace contained a cryptogram.

Cryptogram of Olivier Levasseur:

It is **not** known what happened to the necklace. The cryptogram appears to be written in a script similar to Pigpen (see Chapter 3), but it has **not** been deciphered. Levasseur's treasure is reputedly worth over $1 billion, and while many people have searched, it has **not** yet been found.

Grave of Olivier Levasseur in Saint-Paul, Réunion:

Babington Plot Ciphers

The 16th century was a time of great political intrigue in England. One such intrigue was the Babington Plot of 1586. This was a plan to assassinate the then reigning monarch Queen Elizabeth I (who was a Protestant) and place her cousin Mary, Queen of Scots (who was a Roman Catholic) on the throne instead.

The Babington Plot is named after one of the conspirators, Anthony Babington. The plot was discovered Sir Francis Walsingham who was working for Elizabeth. On July 7th, 1586, an enciphered letter sent by Babington to Mary was intercepted and deciphered by one of Walsingham's agents, Thomas Phelippes. Babington's letter was however allowed to reach Mary, and she responded, also in code, on July 17th. Walsingham and Phelippes then intercepted Mary's reply. Walsingham and Phelippes kept Mary's reply, and passed on a copy with an additional postscript requesting that Babington reveal the names of the conspirators.

Forged postscript of letter by Mary Queen of Scots (top) and Babington's record of the cipher used (bottom):

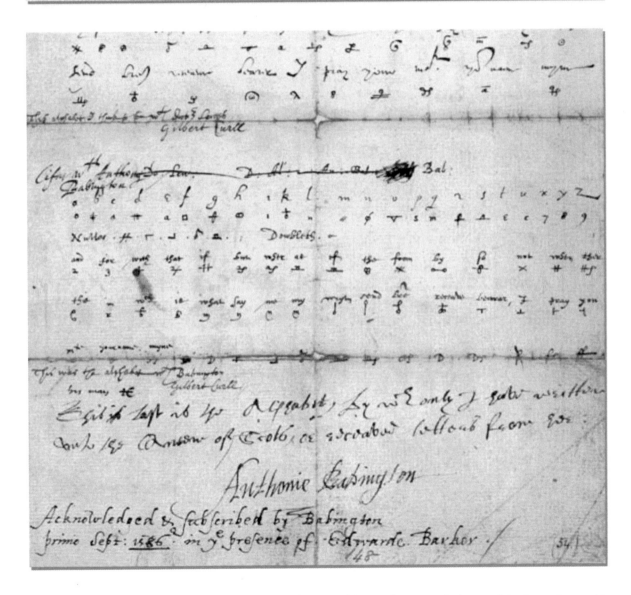

Ultimately fourteen conspirators (including Anthony Babington) were tried, convicted, sentenced to death, and executed. Mary, Queen of Scots was also tried for treason at Fotheringhay Castle in Northamptonshire in October 1586 by a panel of 46 English lords, earls and bishops. Only 1 of the

46 favored a not guilty verdict, and Mary was sentenced to death and executed by beheading on February 8th, 1587.

Shugborough Inscription

The Shugborough Inscription is a sequence of letters carved on Shepherd's Monument which is in the grounds of Shugborough Hall in Staffordshire, England. It appears below a carved mirror image of Nicolas Poussin's painting, the *Shepherds of Arcadia*. The carving has several changes from the the painting, and above the painting are two stone heads, one of a smiling bald man, and the other of the Greek god Pan.

Shepherd's Monument was constructed in the mid-18th century between 1748 and 1763 after being commissioned by Thomas Anson (c. 1695 to March 30th, 1773), who was a British member of parliament, amateur architect, and traveler.

Shugborough Inscription:

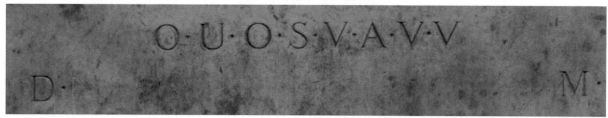

Josiah Wedgwood, Charles Darwin and Charles Dickens are all thought to have attempted to decipher the text but failed. Many possible explanations have since been proposed, some of which are **acrostic** (in which each letter is thought to be the initial letter of a word), but, as yet, there is no definitive explanation.   Among the more exotic theories, is that the inscription is linked to the Holy Grail (the blood of Jesus) – an idea which was first suggested in the book, *The Holy Blood and the Holy Grail* by Baigent, Leigh and Lincoln, and which was later also taken-up in the best-selling novel, *The Da Vinci Code* by Dan Brown.

Copiale Cipher

The Copiale Cipher is an enciphered manuscript of 105 pages in a bound volume, containing approximately 75,000 characters. The character symbols include Greek and Roman characters as well as abstract symbols. There are only two short phrases written in plain text: "Copiales 3" at the end and "Philipp 1866" on the flyleaf.

The Copiale Cipher remained undeciphered for over 260 years. When it was examined by scientists at the German Academy of Sciences in the 1970s, they thought it dated to between 1760 and 1780. The cipher was eventually cracked in 2011 by an international effort using modern computer techniques. The Copiale Cipher is now known to be a document created by a secret society of oculists (medical practitioners specializing in the diagnosis and treatment of diseases of the eye) in the 1730s.

Two pages from the Copiale Cipher:

The text in the Copiale Cipher is German encoded using a substitution cipher (see Chapter 3). However, it does **not** use a simple one-for-one substitution cipher, but instead is homophonic: each plaintext character can be encoded in multiple different ways. For example:

- All unaccented Roman characters represent a space.
- There are seven different ciphertext characters that represent the letter "e".
- Some ciphertext characters stand for a group of plaintext characters such as "sch" or even an entire word such as the name of the secret society.

The Gold-Bug

The Gold-Bug is a short story written by the American author Edgar Allen Poe (January 19th, 1809 to October 7th, 1849). The story, which was first published in 1843, can best be described as an early example of detective fiction and concerns deciphering a secret message in order to find a buried treasure.

The Gold-Bug was extremely successful and popular during Poe's lifetime, and won the grand prize of $100 in a writing contest sponsored by the *Philadelphia Dollar Newspaper*. In the 19th century, *The Gold-Bug* was among the most widely read of Poe's works, and its success helped popularize cryptographic ideas and bring them to the attention of a wider audience. In fact, the story was so successful that it even inspired a stage adaptation which was opened at the American Theatre in Philadelphia on August 8th, 1843. However, to modern audiences the story may be less appealing, as the story's depiction of an African-American character, Jupiter, is now widely considered to be racist.

Edgar Allen Poe:

Cryptography is central to the story of *The Gold-Bug*, and the text includes a complete cryptogram (encoded using a simple substitution cipher) as well as a detailed description of how to use frequency analysis to break substitution ciphers.

The cryptogram from *The Gold-Bug*:

53‡‡†305))6*;4826)4‡.)4‡);806*;48†8¶60))85;1‡)
;:‡*8†83(88)5*†;46(;88*96*?;8)*‡(;485);5*†2:*‡(;4
956*2(5*—4)8¶8*;4069285);)6†8)4‡‡;1(‡9;48081;
8:8‡1;48†85;4)485†528806*81(‡9;48;(88;4(‡?34;48
)4‡;161;:188;‡?;

After deciphering and adding spaces and punctuation, the cryptogram reads:

A good glass in the bishop's hostel in the devil's seat

forty-one degrees and thirteen minutes northeast and by north

main branch seventh limb east side

shoot from the left eye of the death's-head

a bee line from the tree through the shot fifty feet out.

Beale Ciphers

The Beale Ciphers (also known as The Beale Papers) are a set of three cryptograms which were published in a pamphlet in the 19th century. The cryptograms supposedly concern the location of buried treasure of gold, silver and jewels, that is worth tens of millions of dollars:

- The first cryptogram supposedly reveals the location of the treasure, although it has **not** yet been deciphered.
- The second cryptogram, which is deciphered within the pamphlet itself, describes the contents of the treasure.
- The third cryptogram, which like the first has **not** yet been deciphered, supposedly reveals the treasure's owners and their next of kin.

The story begins with an 1885 pamphlet describing a treasure supposedly buried by a Thomas J. Beale in the 1820s in Bedford County, Virginia, USA. Beale is claimed to have entrusted a box containing the three cryptograms to a local innkeeper, Robert Morriss. Morriss in turn supposedly did **not** open the box for 23 years, but eventually gave the papers to an unnamed friend. The friend is then supposed to have spent the next two decades trying to decipher the cryptograms, before eventually giving up and eventually allowing a second friend, James B. Ward, to publish the pamphlet.

Each of the cryptograms is simply a list of one-, two-, three- and four-digit numbers. The second cryptogram is enciphered using a variant of the United States Declaration of Independence (albeit with some mistakes occurring during the enciphering process). The numbers in this cryptogram correspond to positions of words in the Declaration of Independence: the plaintext is the first letter of the referenced word.

Cover of *The Beale Papers*:

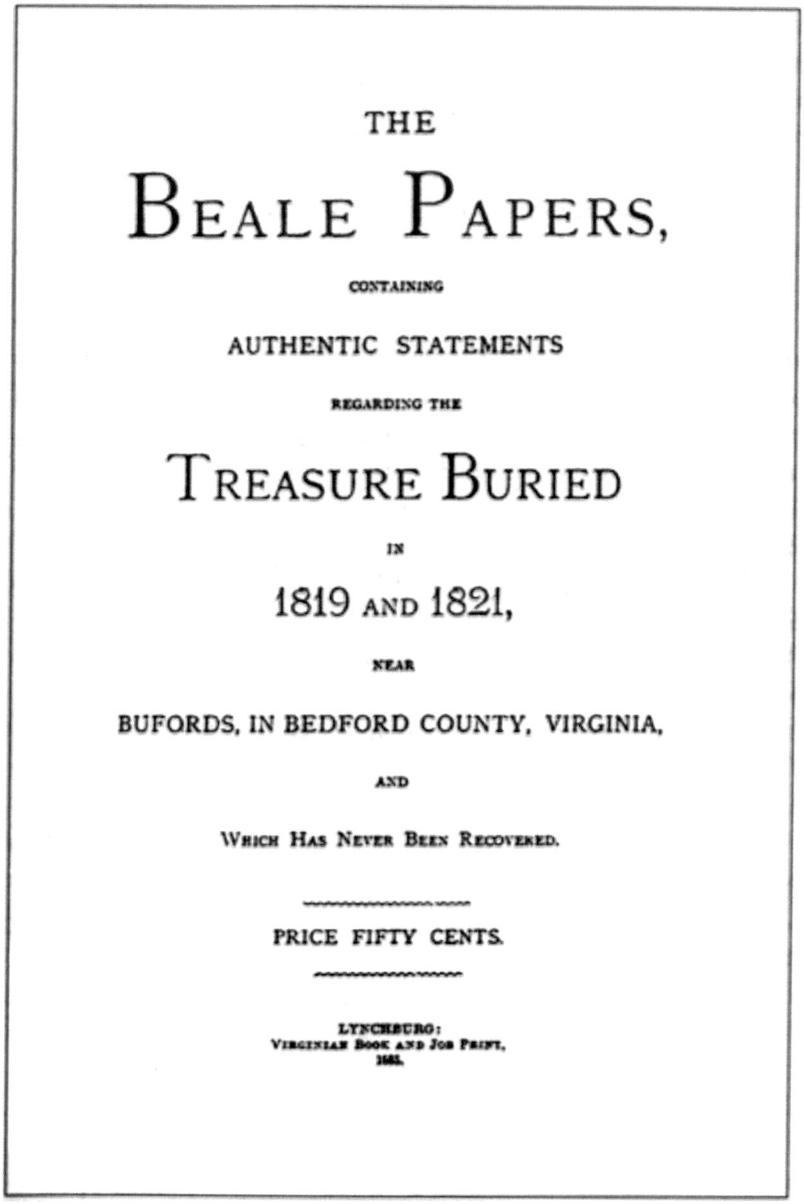

THE

BEALE PAPERS,

CONTAINING

AUTHENTIC STATEMENTS

REGARDING THE

TREASURE BURIED

IN

1819 AND 1821,

NEAR

BUFORDS, IN BEDFORD COUNTY, VIRGINIA,

AND

WHICH HAS NEVER BEEN RECOVERED.

‒‒‒‒‒‒‒‒‒‒

PRICE FIFTY CENTS.

‒‒‒‒‒‒‒‒‒‒

LYNCHBURG:
VIRGINIAN BOOK AND JOB PRINT,
1885.

There are good reasons to believe that the entire story may be a hoax. These reasons include:
- Beale's letters use words like "stampede" and "improvise" that were **not** in use in the 1820s.
- The linguistic style of Beale's letters resembles that of the pamphlet's author (probably James B. Ward), suggesting they were both written by the same person.
- Historians who have searched records for Thomas J. Beale, are doubtful of his existence.

- The pamphlet states that Robert Morriss was running the Washington Hotel in 1820, but historical records show that he was **not** doing so until at least 1823.
- It seems strange that Beale was real that he would use three different cryptograms, each enciphered differently, to transmit what is essentially one message.
- Only the second cryptogram, describing the treasure, has been deciphered: Some people have speculated that this was a calculated measure to increase sales of the pamphlet, which was being sold for the then relatively expensive price of $0.50.
- If Beale wanted to ensure the next of kin received their share of the treasure, it would **not** serve his purpose to encipher the third cryptogram.
- The length of the third cryptogram appears to be too short for the number of names supposedly contained within it.
- The first and third cryptograms seem to have statistical characteristics unlike those of English text. Additionally, if the Declaration of Independence is used with the first cryptogram, it yields strings like *abfdefghiijklmmnohpp*, which are unlikely to have arisen by chance, but do suggest that that the first cryptogram may **not** contain an English message.

Although there are good reasons to believe the entire thing may be a hoax, people have continued to look for the treasure. Attempts to decipher the first and third cryptograms continue to this day, and some people have even gone hunting for the treasure.

Rohonc Codex

The Rohonc Codex is a manuscript book containing text in an unknown language and writing system. The origins of the codex are unknown, but the first definitive records of its existence are in Hungary in the early 19th century. The codex is named after the city of Rohonc in western Hungary (today Rechnitz in Austria) where It was kept until 1838.

A facsimile of the Rohonc Codex:

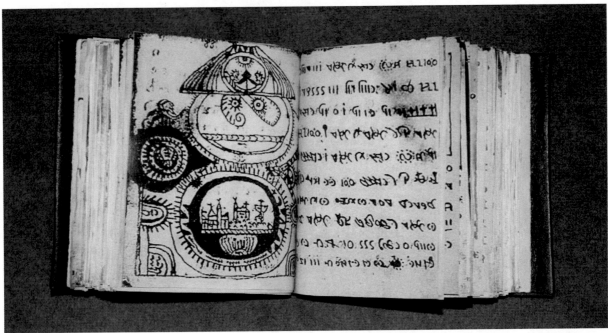

The codex contains 448 pages, some with illustrations. The pages each contain between 9 and 14 rows of symbols. There are many different types of symbols (approximately 800), and some of the symbols appear rarely, so it is **not** clear whether they represent alphabetic characters. Based on the formatting, the symbols appear to be written right to left.

A page from the Rohonc Codex:

Both scholars and amateurs have studied the codex, but no definite conclusion has yet been reached. Many Hungarian scholars are of the opinion that the codex is an 18th century hoax.

D'Agapeyeff Cipher

The D'Agapeyeff Cipher is a sequence of 5-digit numbers that is offered as a "challenge" ciphertext. It appears at the end of the first edition of a 1939 book by Alexander D'Agapeyeff which is entitled *Codes and Ciphers*.

The cipher does **not** appear in subsequent editions of the book, and D'Agapeyeff supposedly said that he had forgotten how he enciphered it. *Codes and Ciphers* discusses Polybius squares (see Chapter 1) and null characters (see Chapter 3), so it may be that these methods were used to encipher the message. However, despite many attempts, the D'Agapeyeff Cipher remains unbroken to this day.

Dorabella Cipher

The Dorabella Cipher is a cryptogram written in 1897 by the composer Edward Elgar (June 2nd, 1857 to February 23rd, 1934) to Dora Penny (1874 to 1964). At the time, Elgar was Dora's music teacher, and although Dora was many years younger than him, the two liked each other and remained friends for the rest of Elgar's life.

Edward Elgar:

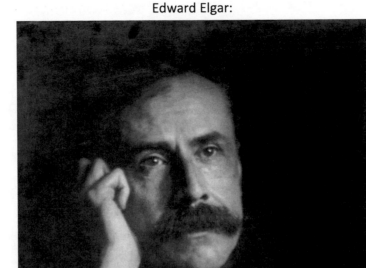

Elgar sent Dora an enciphered letter accompanied by another unenciphered letter dated July 14th, 1897. The ciphertext contains 87 character-symbols in three lines. The symbols consist of one, two or three semicircles orientated in various directions, and there is also a small dot after the fifth symbol on the third line.

An image of the Dorabella ciphertext:

Dora Penny was never able to decipher the message herself. Various explanations have been proposed by others, including that an English message is encoded in a simple substitution cipher (two entirely different clear text messages have been suggested) or that the symbols include **not** text but a melody. None of these explanations have been universally accepted, and in 2007 the Elgar Society held a competition to decipher the message. The 2007 competition yielded a number of entries, but none of them were found satisfactory by the judges.

Zimmerman Telegram

In 1914, World War I broke out between the Entente Powers (including Britain, France, Russia, Japan and later Italy) and the Central Powers (including Germany, Austria-Hungary and the Ottoman Empire). War raged across Europe. At sea, the German economy was being slowly strangled by a British naval blockade.

Germany's declared exclusion around the United Kingdom as of February 18th, 1915. Merchant ships within the zone were liable to search and attack.

Beginning in 1915, German U-boats conducted a campaign of unrestricted submarine warfare against Entente shipping. German U-boats attacked merchantmen without warning. The most famous incident of this type was the 1915 sinking of the British liner RMS *Lusitania* with the loss of 1,198 lives including 128 US citizens.

The sinking of RMS *Lusitania* caused an international outcry and led to Germany fearing that the United States would enter the war on the Entente side. On September 9th, 1915, Germany announced that attacks would only be made on ships that were definitely British, that neutral ships would be treated under the Prize Law (also known as the Cruiser Rules) in which the ship is searched and the crew taken to safety before sinking, and that no passenger ships would be attacked at all.

The New York Times front page on May 8th, 1915:

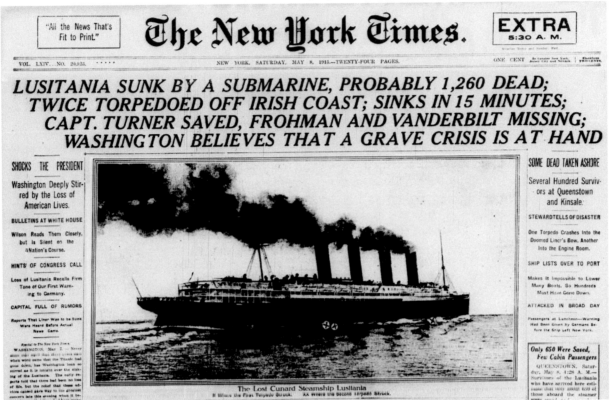

By 1917, the effects of the British naval blockade and the stalemate of trench warfare on the Western Front led the Germans to look for other alternative strategies. German Admiral Henning von Holtzendorff argued successfully for full unrestricted submarine warfare against the British. Although Holtzendorff did **not** believe that the US would join the war, the German high command assumed it would, but calculated that Britain would be defeated before the US could decisively intervene.

As part of its preparations for possible war with the United States, Germany had been meddling in Mexican affairs since 1914 and actively trying to foment a war between the US and Mexico since 1915. On January 16th, 1917, Arthur Zimmerman (October 5th, 1864 to June 6th, 1940), who was State Secretary for Foreign Affairs of the German Empire, sent a coded telegram to the German ambassador to Mexico, Heinrich von Eckardt (July 20th, 1861 to March 3rd, 1944). The telegram instructed Eckardt to seek a military alliance between Mexico and Germany against the United States, with an offer of German funding and Mexican annexation of the US states of Arizona, New Mexico and Texas. The telegram also suggested that Japan (even though it was a member of the Entente) would be invited to join the alliance, although it did **not** state what Japan would receive in return.

Arthur Zimmerman:

The German's own telegraphic cables had been cut by the Entente at the start of the war, but the US had agreed to allow Germany to use their cables to communicate with the German ambassador in Washington DC. The Germans therefore delivered the coded message to the United States embassy in Berlin, who in turn passed it to the US embassy in Denmark, which then transmitted the message to Washington. The Germans plan was that once the message had been received by their ambassador in Washington, it would be retransmitted to Eckardt, their ambassador in Mexico City.

However, unbeknownst to both the Germans and Americans, since the American cable passed through a relay station near Porthcurno in England, the British were eavesdropping on American diplomatic traffic. British cryptanalyst, Nigel de Grey (March 27th, 1886 to May 25th, 1951), working in Room 40 of the Admiralty, had partially deciphered the message by the next day, and together with William Montgomery (1871 to 1930) produced a complete decryption within three weeks.

The Zimmerman telegram as sent (left) and decrypted and translated into English (right):

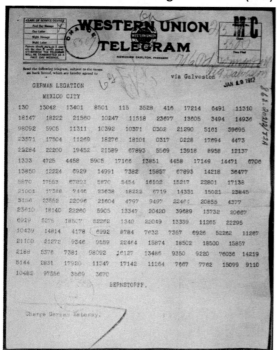

The British struggled with a way to reveal the contents of the telegram without revealing that they were eavesdropping on US diplomatic cables, or that they had broken German codes. To do this, they put about various disinformation stories and also bribed an employee of the Mexican telegraph office for a second copy of the message when it was transmitted by the Germans through that country. The Germans also made the mistake of retransmitting the message in an older code, which meant at worst the Germans would think the British had broken their older code. When the message was eventually revealed, the Germans never considered the possibility that their cipher had been broken, and instead searched their embassy in Mexico for a traitor.

In mid-February, the British revealed the telegram and its contents to officials in the US Embassy in London. American officials were enraged by the German duplicity and passed the information to US President Woodrow Wilson (December 28th, 1856 to February 3rd, 1924). Wilson then revealed the information to the media on February 28th, 1917. As a result of the resumption of the unrestricted submarine warfare and the Zimmerman telegram, the United States entered the war against Germany on April 6th, 1917.

Newspaper cartoon about the Zimmerman telegram:

Zodiac Killer Ciphers

The Zodiac Killer was a serial killer active in Northern California in the late 1960s and possibly into the early 1970s. He is known to have had at least seven victims, two of whom survived, and claimed to have had up to 37 victims.

San Francisco Police Department sketch of the Zodiac Killer:

The name "Zodiac" comes from a series of letters sent by the killer to the San Francisco Bay Area press. The letters included four cryptograms, encoded using a combination of letters and letter-like symbols. Out of the four, only the first has been definitely deciphered.

The story of the letters begins on August 1st, 1969, when three nearly identical letters written by the killer were received by the *San Francisco Chronicle*, *The San Francisco Examiner* and the *Vallejo Times Herald*. Each letter was accompanied by one-third of a 408-symbol cryptogram (sometimes subsequently referred to as "Z 408"). The killer demanded be printed on the newspaper's front page or else he would "cruse [sic] around all weekend killing lone people in the night then move on to kill again, until I end up with a dozen people over the weekend."

On August 2nd, the *San Francisco Chronicle* published the letter that it had received on page 4. The letter was accompanied by an article quoting the Vallejo Police Chief stating, "We're not satisfied that the letter was written by the murderer" and requesting that the letter writer prove his identity.

On August 7th, a further letter was received by *The San Francisco Examiner*. In this letter, the killer identified himself as "Zodiac", provided details of the murders that had **not** been released to the public, and a note to the police saying "By the way, are the police haveing [sic] a good time with the code? If not, tell them to cheer up; when they do crack it they will have me.".

When the threatened murder rampage did **not** occur, all three parts of the cryptogram were eventually published. The three-part cryptogram was broken on August 8th by North Salinas schoolteacher Donald Harden and his wife Bettye. When deciphered, the message explained that the killer was collecting slaves for the afterlife, and that he would **not** give away his identity ("I WILL NOT GIVE YOU MY NAME") so as **not** to slow down or stop the slave collection process.

Bettye Harden came up with the key idea for breaking the code: she guessed some words that were likely to appear in the cryptograms (cribs). Given the killer's apparent quest for attention, Bettye correctly guessed that that the message would begin with the word "I". She also guessed the message would somewhere contain the word "KILL" or "KILLING", or the phrase "I LIKE KILLING". Both of Bettye's guesses were correct.

First Zodiac Killer Cipher deciphered by Donald and Bettye Harden:

 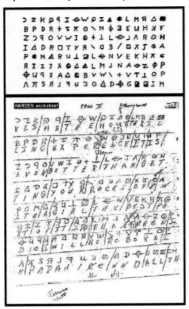 

Zodiac sent another letter (unenciphered) to the *San Francisco Chronicle* in October. Later that same month, somebody claiming to be Zodiac made a phone call to the Oakland Police Department and several calls to a local television show, *A.M. San Francisco*.

The second cryptogram was mailed on November 8th. This cryptogram contained a message of 340 characters (and is sometimes referred to as "Z 340"), and despite decades of effort by amateurs and professionals has never yet been definitively deciphered.

In 2017, a possible partial solution to Z 340 was proposed by Craig P. Bauer, who is professor of mathematics at York College of Pennsylvania. Bauer's proposed solution was publicized by The History Channel in *The Hunt for the Zodiac Killer*. Bauer suggested that the cipher was a substitution cipher with homophony (see Chapter 3) where each plaintext character can be translated into several different ciphertext characters. However, Bauer's proposed solution is controversial as it does **not** produce a clear deciphered message, leaves out some ciphertext characters, interprets the same ciphertext character in different ways in different places, adds some plaintext characters, and deciphers the latter part of the message into gibberish.

The card received by the *San Francisco Chronicle*, mailed on November 8th, 1969:

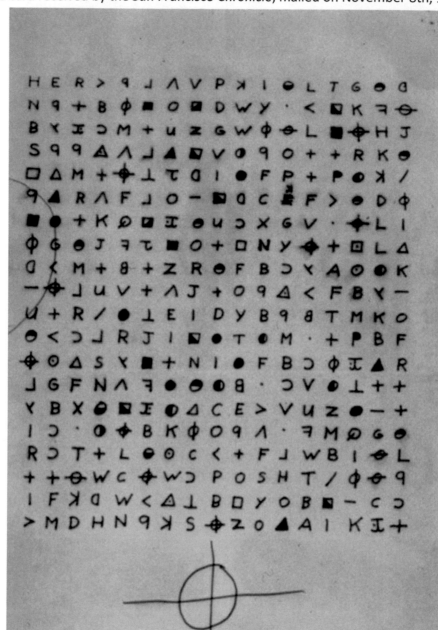

Later in 1969 and through 1970, Zodiac continued to send letters and greeting cards many of which were signed with the crosshair-like symbol previously seen on the bottom of Z 340. In a letter that was sent on April 20th, 1970, Zodiac wrote "My name is _____," followed by a 13-character ciphertext (referred to as "Z 13").

Because it is so short, there are numerous possible interpretations of Z 13. However, it has been noted that one possibility is that the ciphertext encodes "ALFRED E. NEUMAN", the mascot of the satirical *Mad* magazine. This hypothesis is supported by the fact that the first three letters of the ciphertext are "AEN", which are of course the same initials.

Zodiac letter sent April 20th, 1970:

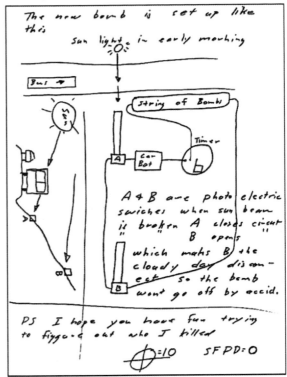

Zodiac's final ciphertext (referred to as "Z 32") was contained in a letter sent on June 26th, 1970. With the letter was a roadmap of the San Francisco area, and drawn on the map over Mount Diablo was a "compass" resembling his crosshair-like symbol but surrounded by the digits "0", "3", "6" and "9". In this letter, Zodiac claimed that have buried a bomb. In the letter, he stated "0 is to be set to Mag. N" and explained that the combination of map and cipher would lead to the bomb. To date, Z 32 has **not** been deciphered and neither has the alleged bomb exploded or been found.

Zodiac letter sent on June 26th, 1970:

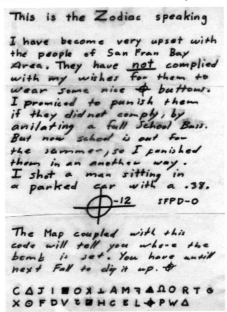

Zodiac would continue to send letters for several more years. The last letter definitely attributed to Zodiac was sent to The San Francisco Chronicle on January 29th, 1974 and included a strange symbol at the bottom that has never been explained. Additionally, there are a handful of other letters sent later in the 1970s and a Christmas card postmarked 1990 which have been attributed by some to Zodiac, although others disagree with this assessment.

Zodiac's letter dated January 29th, 1974:

The Magic Words are Squeamish Ossifrage

Multiplying two large prime numbers (whole numbers which are only divisible by themselves and 1) to produce a number known as a semiprime is much easier than starting with a semiprime and factorizing it to produce two prime numbers. RSA (Rivest-Shamir-Adleman) is a public key encryption system (see Chapter 12) that relies upon this fact.

The RSA algorithm was first published in 1977. In the same year, the creators issued a challenge to decipher a ciphertext generated using a 129-digit semiprime. At the time, Ron Rivest, one of the creators of RSA, estimated it would take over 40,000,000,000,000,000 years to factorize the number and decipher text using the best algorithms and fastest computers then available. However, he did also recommend using 200-digit semiprimes for protection against future developments.

The text was deciphered in 1993-4 in a collaborative computer effort involving 600 volunteers and over 1,600 computers. After six months work, the volunteers revealed that the message read "The Magic Words are Squeamish Ossifrage". "Ossifrage" is Latin for "bone-breaker" and a reference to the bearded vulture (*Gypaetus barbatus*) which breaks animal bones by dropping them onto rocks.

In 2015, the feat of factorizing the 129-digit semiprime was repeated using a commercial cloud computing service at a cost of just US $30. Larger RSA semiprimes have also been factorized since 1993-4, the largest of these being 240 digits long. To avoid the risk of factorization (and hence somebody deciphering secret messages), larger RSA numbers are now used, the largest currently in use (as of early 2020) being 617 digits long.

Kryptos

Kryptos is a sculpture created by the American artist Jim Sanborn. It is located in the grounds of the Central Intelligence Agency (CIA) in Langley, Virginia, USA. The sculpture contains four cryptograms, only three of which have been deciphered to date. Two of the deciphered cryptograms are enciphered using a Vigenère cipher (see Chapter 7) and the third uses a transposition cipher (see Chapter 4). It is **not** known what method of encryption has been used for the fourth cipher.

Part of Kryptos:

Ricky McCormick's Encrypted Notes

Ricky McCormick was a 41-year-old homicide victim who lived in St. Charles County, Missouri, USA. The last time McCormick was definitely seen alive was on June 25th, 1999 at the emergency room at Forest Park hospital after he had an asthma flare-up. On the morning of June 26th, he spoke on the phone to his girlfriend Sandra Jones, and on the following day he is believed to have been seen by a gas-station worker at a local Amoco.

Soon after these events Ricky McCormick was dead. His body was found in a cornfield about 15 miles (24 kilometers) from his home. How he got there is a mystery, as McCormick did **not** drive and the area was **not** served by public transportation.

Three notes were found in McCormick's jeans pockets, although investigators choose **not** to reveal this until 12 years later. Two of the notes consist of a jumble of letters, apparently written in an unknown code.

Note 1 (left) and note 2 (right):

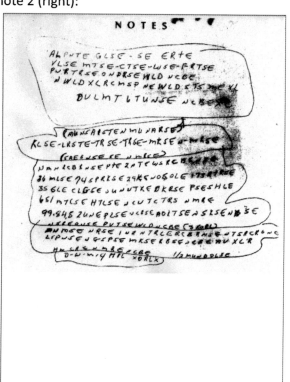

The FBI have suggested that deciphering the notes could potentially explain McCormick's whereabouts before his death and perhaps solve the case. Whether, McCormick himself wrote the notes is also something of a mystery, as his family have said he had very limited writing abilities and lacked the capacity to write such notes. The FBI however believe that McCormick did write the notes, probably for this own private consumption, perhaps as an aide-mémoire to himself.

To date both the FBI's Cryptanalysis and Racketeering Records Unit (CRRU) and the American Cryptogram Association have been unable to decipher the notes. The notes are today listed by the CRRU as one of their top unsolved cases, and the FBI have even created a webpage, https://forms.fbi.gov/code, which allows members of the public to submit comments and hypotheses about the case.

Smithy Code

In 2006, Michael Baigent and Richard Leigh, two of the authors of *The Holy Blood and the Holy Grail* sued Random House, the publishers of Dan Brown's *The Da Vinci Code*. Baigent and Leigh alleged that Brown's book plagiarized their work and thus infringed their copyright. Eventually however, the presiding judge, Mr Justice Peter Smith, ruled that since Baigent and Leigh had presented their ideas as fact, a novelist must be free to use these ideas in a fictional context.

In April 2006, the approved final judgement of the case was issued. Concealed within the 71-page judgement was a cryptogram that Smith had included for his own amusement. At apparently random places within the judgement, certain letters were italicized. When extracted these italicized letters read:

s m i t h y c o d e J a e i e x t o s t g p s a c g r e a m q w f k a d p m q z v

The code was eventually broken by Dan Tench, a lawyer who works for The Guardian newspaper, after he received a series of clues from Smith via email. The message was encoded using a Variant Beaufort Cipher (see Chapter 7), and the deciphered message reads:

JACKIEFISTERWHOAREYOUDREADNOUGH

It seems that Smith made some errors when enciphering the message, as the intended message was a reference to the British admiral Jackie Fisher (note: the "T" instead of "H" in the cryptogram). Fisher is known for being one of the key figures in the development of the first modern battleship, HMS *Dreadnought* (note: the final "T" of *Dreadnought* is missing in the cryptogram).

Conclusion

Well done for getting to the end. I hope you enjoyed this book!

For related resources and more information about codes, ciphers and secret messages, please go to: http://www.suniltanna.com/codes

If you enjoyed this book or it helped you, please post a positive review on Amazon!

I have written many other books.
- To find out about other books that I have written, please go to: http://www.suniltanna.com/
- For computing books: http://www.suniltanna.com/computing
- For math books: http://www.suniltanna.com/math
- For science books: http://www.suniltanna.com/science

P.S.

Here are three cryptograms, starting easy and gradually getting harder, for you to decipher. Feel free to challenge your family, friends and Facebook friends too! **If you solved them, be sure to mention it in your Amazon review!** (but please do **not** post the deciphered messages so as **not** to spoil the fun for other people)

- **Cryptogram 1:** KTZWX HTWJF SIXJA JSDJF WXFLT TZWKF YMJWX GWTZL MYKTW YMTSY MNXHT SYNSJ SYFSJ BSFYN TSHTS HJNAJ INSQN GJWYD FSIIJ INHFY JIYTY MJUWT UTXNY NTSYM FYFQQ RJSFW JHWJF YJIJV ZFQST BBJFW JJSLF LJINS FLWJF YHNAN QBFWY JXYNS LBMJY MJWYM FYSFY NTSTW FSDSF YNTSX THTSH JNAJI FSIXT IJINH FYJIH FSQTS LJSIZ WJBJF WJRJY TSFLW JFYGF YYQJX K NJQIT KYMFY BFWBJ MFAJ TRJYT IJINH FYJFU TWYNT STKYM FYKNJ QIFXF KNSFQ WJXYN SLUQF HJKTW YMTXJ BMTMJ WJLFA JYMJN WQNAJ XYMFY YMFY SFYNT SRNLMY QNAJ YNXFQ YTLJY MJWKN SIUWT UJWFY YFWYM XMTZQ IITYM NXGZY SFQFW WIJWX JSXJB JHFSS TYITS XYFYJ BJHFS STYHT SXJHW FYJBJ HFSST YMFQQ TBYMN XLWTZ SIYMJ GWFAJ RJSQN ANSLF SIIFJ IMFAJ HTSXJ HWFYJ IN YKFWF GTAJT ZWUTT WUTBJ WYTFII TWIJY WFHYY MJWTQ IWTWI FJKWT RYMJX JMTST WJIIF IBJYF GJBNY GMFYY MFYBJ MJWJM NLMQD WJXTQ AJYMF YYMJX JIJFI XMFQQ STYMF AJINJ INSAF NSYMF YYMNX SFYNT SZSIJ WLTIX MFQQM FAJFS JBGNW YMTKK WJJIT RFSIY MFYLT AJWSR JSYTK YMJUJ TUQJG DYMJU JTUQJ KTWYM JUJTU QJXMF QQSTY UJWNX MKWTR YMJJF WYM

Cryptogram continues…

- **Cryptogram 2:** QIGPY VYOQI IQIOO JXWMY UGYXG PYPYU EYIUI XGPYY UMGPU IXGPY YUMGP DUNDQ GPJFG ZJMHU IXEJQ XUIXX UMSIY NNDUN FKJIG PYZUW YJZGP YXXYYK UIXGP YNKQM QGJZO JXHJE YXFKJ IGPYZ UWYJZ GPYDU GYMNU IXGPJ XNUDG PYHQH PYSPU GYDUJ FUHPU NUXHU GJQSY IGPJX NUDGP YHQHP YSPUG YDUJF UHPUN UXHUG JQSYI GPJXN UDGPY HQHPY SPUGY DUJFU HPUNU XHUGJ QSYIG PJXNU DGPYH QHPYS PUGYD UJFUH PUNUX HUGJQ SYIGP JXNUD GPYHQ HPYSP UGYDU JFUHP UNUXH UGJQS YIXGP YHQHP YSPUG YDUJF UHPUN UXHUG JQSYI GPJXN UDGPY HQHPY SPUGY DUJFU HPUNU XHUGJ QSYI

- **Cryptogram 3:** YVHRK BWLGQ RYTGH SHVXQ CBHZG BWWKH EIECP IUBHG GGVET MISTC QIRSR TNSWS FWVWQ ZYIVV HTQZL XKQDP DOQHU KKMEV KEXSF SPBHG VSGXJ SPAKH KEPCW LGFDR FHREU GXQGO PSPUW LGDRA GFVSH HKIGO UXJHK IUSSE TOWIC BGISI DPUHD XKCQX QKKME VWLGZ DAUCI RCHXV GOQHQ TQEVI UIUUR HGBWM VZHXJ SPEFS FIPHU IUDHG VHRXJ SRTKB LSPGR JOOQO KBGVG EXMTS VXJOW XJSBW JCXPF RHGNO UIVVH GCIVI UKKME VLQRS OXJSP XQHKI USSET OWMQB ZIJCO HVVHW GHUYV VVXQP HWGZI IXWGI PHWLC HDPNA HRCFH GTSDX GRHUW OOXJO WXJSB ETSHR FCZIF PBXJS LVEFH EVCUA KHKGG FWEKB XRCZL IPOEP GFLKJ HVXJO WEOCQ KVVHW GOUIN WIINW EITHB EPRWL GDXVU ILXQT KERDL RGGVX JOWXQ GHGWF HXJSV ITWJL VGJSX SUROS QXUOU IKBVX KHXXG RDQQB JQGBG ITWYM PUWLG WUNWG WTQKH VUTUS OHKIE CQWGB WSHHK IICYI TBHHV VDXYV HRGJH VCBBJ QFPSH URZGF QQGBW FGQRQ GGGIU HUYEH LZGCI XJSVI GBGWK HLWVV HVKUK XQTWL GDHSR ZHXQO OXGFR VVCDF QZLWJ WWEPR WSKBV XKHXX GBHAI CYITB PIPHO EAWQK KHVJQ IQHCH LSPCQ WWQKT TWQGK DOIUO QHQFJ EPWCM PULXU DRAGF VMPGX GJTRV OOVXQ HKIOG KENZV IGAPS UHOMM SOCVC HJHSF XVVHM TGDJG HBEPR KERDL RGGVT TIGIP QHMPR HIFKL PNRLG VOWIV VDXIC YITBP IPHVP QBJIU HDFNW VLGRV LQIOH PCWFG QKEPU HHHCU PKUKX CBGXT OQWKS QXEOX WGGDR FOFGQ FGMPU OCCZO IZDHV KSQGG VDXJG KIYBW LCHPE PYLRF OUIOC UIFWV TQGHH VCVYH THVYV LPGSY MNGDV GGXJH SUEDZ HXJOQ XQFLK JHWLG AVINJ HWDMD FQZLW JWQKV VHJQF PWVCZ LKQKX JSBET SDGEI VXQAH HDIWA JSQEN CQKVF DMPCI EDIVI UOQHW GXVRO WMQBV TWFVY KBJMP JDVKO EPAHK IUOPI QPMIE HHZKB FIUOG IUWJR VCUIF IFIVV HQWBG ITOEW QZXXG RHWRC WMUAL XKGWL GWUVK UKXKH LWVVH MTRXX AHRXJ FRAQT IWWQK KQJHV PAHRV OQHVC SVQJL HGBHA IIDVF GISTH KIKFI YVIUI USFYT WWCUI FLJOV FGSQX JSSEV WHRVG XJHSU EPQHS HHKIU SFSNC QMGGD RFGXG JWVRQ KWLGB HGGGV MVMZL KQKGQ BVXTO LRUHK IOHRE NHHVV VHMTT RVOSU WAGWI OGRJI CYITB PIPHW LGVLW VCUCQ TWLGD UIUSQ XMWQK QTJVG OWFTW WEKBL WCVLW VCUCQ TUIRS DXGRL RLIUM GGDRF IVYTD DXKCQ WCZOL CJLRI WQHKF HGVCE NGQWX JSHWV OEPKG KQGBW SHOQE DGRPW HHXAF DRPMR ZGFWL GGHWV OWIUH RTTCY IVVLW NSWJC QWWDS VYDAL XVSGX QOFEP RLHYCUPF